TOTAL QUALITY MANAGEMENT
Performance and Cost Measures:
The Strategy for Economic Survival

TOTAL QUALITY MANAGEMENT
Performance and Cost Measures:
The Strategy for Economic Survival

Dorsey J. Talley

ASQC Quality Press

TOTAL QUALITY MANAGEMENT
Performance and Cost Measures
The Strategy for Economic Survival

Dorsey J. Talley

Library of Congress Cataloging-in-Publication Data
Talley, Dorsey J.
    Total quality management : performance and cost measures : the
strategy for economic survival / Dorsey J. Talley.
        p.   cm.
    Includes bibliographical references.
    ISBN 0-87389-095-7
    1. Quality of products—Measurement. 2. Industrial productivity—
Measurement. I. Title.
    HF6415.157.T35   1991   90-27245
    658.5′62—dc20   CIP

10 9 8 7 6 5 4 3 2 1

ISBN 0-87389-095-7

Acquisitions Editor: Jeanine L. Lau
Production Editor: Tammy Griffin
Set in Baskerville by Carlisle Communications. Cover design by Cathy Chojnacki.
Printed and bound by BookCrafters.

Printed in the United States of America
ASQC Quality Press
310 West Wisconsin Avenue
Milwaukee, Wisconsin 53203

To Norma Jean

Contents

Achievers Lead
Visionary Leadership
Enterprise Education
Barriers to TQM
A President's Checklist
Summary

Foreword

The most talked about, the most important, and probably the most poorly implemented improvement strategy is measurement. We are not talking about product-related measurement. We do a fair job of measuring yields, defects per unit, percent defective, supplier lots rejected, etc. What we are talking about is customer-related measurement of our products and services, as well as internal measurement of our support groups' efficiency, effectiveness, and adaptability.

Measurement is the key ingredient in any improvement process. If you cannot measure it, you cannot control it. If you cannot control it, you cannot manage it—it's as simple as that. Measurement truly separates a successful improvement process from one that fails. The problem is that many areas, departments, and people feel they cannot measure the efficiency and the effectiveness of their activities. If this is true, how do they know who to promote and who to fire? The real problem is that too many managers have lived with the belief that they cannot measure what they manage, and the results have been disastrous. Inefficient, bureaucracy-laden business systems have developed that have not provided acceptable output. Program schedules are modified regularly, orders are lost, bills are paid late, and resources are poorly used.

Everywhere we look in the support areas, we can see waste. Waste runs as high as 80% of budget in some support areas, and 50% is common. The real productivity improvement in the service sector was −6% for the first half of the 1980s compared to +21% for the manufacturing sector. Yes, that's right— our service sector was more productive in the 1970s than it was in the 1980s. Why is the service sector losing ground so much more rapidly than the manufacturing sector? One of the primary reasons is because the service industry and support areas in most organizations have no measurement system, or at best, a poor one. Every job takes an input, adds value to it, and produces an output. The correct measurement system should document how efficiently the value-added content was applied and how well the value-added effort met the users' expectations. If you, your employees, or your area do not add value, there is really no need for your activity and it should be eliminated. If your organization does add value, then it can, should, and must be measured if real, long-lasting improvement is to be made in your quest to become or stay world class.

Although Jim Talley clearly discusses many important quality improvement methods in this book, his greatest contribution rests in his new, organized approach to measurement systems. His approach is a major contribution to the continuous improvement process that has developed over the past 20 years and was instrumental in the TQM process at General Dynamics. This book provides for the first time a definitive roadmap to measuring both the production and support functions. It will help all managers improve the way they perform their present assignment.

In providing measurement criteria for all areas of the business, Jim has eliminated everyone's excuse that they cannot be measured. The list in Appendix A of different measurements by functional organization alone is worth three times the cost of the book. As Lord Kelvin put it, "When you can measure what you are speaking about and express it in numbers, you know something about it, and when you cannot measure it, when you cannot express it in numbers, your knowledge is of a meager and unsatisfactory kind. It may be the beginning of knowledge, but you have scarcely in your thoughts advanced to the stage of a science."

This book not only provides the reader with a list of measurements you can select from; it also provides a methodology that will allow you to expand on Jim's excellent work, modifying it to suit the individual personality of your organization. The book provides a systematic approach that can be applied to design effective measurement systems from the corporate level down to the individual performance plan. It is a book every manager will find useful. It is an important addition to everyone's business library.

H. James Harrington, PhD
International Quality Advisor
Ernst & Young

Herbert F. Rogers
President and Chief Operating Officer
General Dynamics

Preface

Every CEO, president, and manager wants to do better. To continually improve, top management needs to focus on the following major objectives:

- Profits as percent of capital employed (ROI)
- Profits as percent of sales (ROS)
- Sales as a multiple of capital
- Sales as a multiple of fixed assets
- Inventory turnover ratio
- Complaints/grievances per 100 employees
- Suggestions per 100 employees
- Sales per employee
- Profits per employee

Improving performance must be directed at satisfying cross-functional efforts such as quality, productivity, cost, schedule, personnel development, product development, and increased customer satisfaction. To achieve success and attain these important objectives requires a well-designed management information system (MIS). This MIS should contain a measurement system for both performance attainment and accountability for the management team and work groups.

This book is designed to help management and work groups develop measurement methodologies for improving quality, productivity, and overall performance. If you don't know what the costs of unquality (failure costs) are in your organization, then how can you lead them in the improvement direction?

These failure costs, as reported by several quality gurus, can be as high as 30 percent of sales for manufacturing companies, 50 percent of operating expenses for service companies, and 50 percent of operating expenses for software companies. If you cannot measure this type of performance, then how can you manage it!

Go check it out yourself—isn't that what management and leadership are all about?

Acknowledgments

The revolution of quality has begun in the United States. It formally began under the Reagan-Bush administrations with the establishment of the Malcolm Baldrige National Quality Award. The criteria for winning this prestigious award are depicted in Appendix B; information packets on the award are available from the American Productivity Center in Houston, Texas, 713/681-4020.

The Department of Defense (DoD) stepped up past efforts on quality improvement with Dr. Robert Costello, assistant secretary of defense (acquisition), asking for new pressures on cost control and product quality and delivering an unprecedented level of commitment and new vision. Jack Strickland and Frank Dohtery, of the same DoD office, responded with the broad designation of their quality renaissance as Total Quality Management.

General Dynamics and other companies—through the industry associations —responded with all the studies and lessons learned from the past two decades. Fortunately, a number of companies had already anticipated the "quality call." Some of these visionary and world-competitive companies are Boeing, IBM, ITT, Florida Power and Light, Motorola, Ford Westinghouse, and General Dynamics.

Special caveats go to Jim Mayben, Mike Croy, Pat Hayes, and Janet O'Neal of General Dynamics, Fort Worth Division, for reviewing and critiquing the manuscript. And to Mary Harper, executive secretary, special assistant to the vice president, quality assurance, and now, configuration management specialist at General Dynamics, for her extensive work in helping to put this book together.

Thanks.

Talley-ho!

Prologue

Total quality is the driving force to value creation, across all elements of any successful business. I know of nothing more important to our survival and prosperity than quality.[1]

Douglas D. Danworth
Chairman, Westinghouse Electric Corporation

The Quality Manifesto

Declaration

High quality is the key to pride, productivity, and profitability. The quality objective must be products and services that provide customer satisfaction. To be successful, the quality activities must be management led and consumer oriented. Management, labor, and government support for quality improvement is essential for effective competition in the global market place. Control of quality is a strategic business imperative essential to product and service process leadership.

Quality improvement, however, is more than a business strategy — it is a personal responsibility, part of our cultural heritage, and a key source of national pride. Quality commitment is an attitude, formulated in board rooms and living rooms, visible on factory floors and service counters, expressed in concert halls and city halls, and demonstrated on playing fields and wheat fields. Quality demands a continuous improvement process with measurable individual, corporate, and national performance goals. Quality commitment must characterize the best of our relations with our fellow citizens and play a vital role in our search for global cooperation.

Call to Action

With the importance of quality now recognized worldwide, this Quality Manifesto declares that renewed emphasis on quality of both goods and services must be made and maintained as a national priority. Specifically, there is immediate need for the following actions:

~ Leaders of government have the primary responsibility to declare and define the importance of quality as a national priority. They must make clear that quality, which enhances productivity and reduces costs, is the most effective competitive strategy for economic survival and prosperity. All government products and services must be procured and dispensed with a relentless pursuit of quality.

~ Business and labor communities must encourage and intensify their support for quality improvements in all aspects of manufacturing and service operations. They must define the value of products and services in terms of customer satisfaction.

~ The educational community must set higher standards of academic performance and achievement to aid in meeting the expectations of the general public for quality products and services.

~ Professional and trade associations must assist all segments of society in reaching these quality goals. They must provide leadership in the discovery and dissemination of new quality technologies.

~ Individuals must pledge dedication to the attainment, maintenance, and enhancement of quality in all aspects of life.

We the undersigned, all past presidents of the American Society for Quality Control, attest to the urgent need for a renewed and intensified national commitment to quality and issue this Manifesto as a challenge to achieve these ends.

--- May 21, 1986 ---

Ralph E. Wareham
Alfred R. Davis
Paul C. Rohm
Arthur Bender, Jr.
Dale L. Lobsinger
C. Eugene Fisher
J. M. Clure

Rocco L. Fiaschetti
William A. J. Golomski
T. C. McDermott
Thomas E. Turner
Leslie I. Medlock
David S. Clamkey
Richard A. Freund
Larry J. Lessig
Howard L. Stier

Charles H. Brokaw
Walter L. Hurd, Jr.
Jay W. Leek
John D. Hromi
Robert R. Mear
E. J. Thomas
John L. Hansel
H. Harrington

Should We Change?

1

*Extremism in the defense of liberty
is no vice,
Moderation in the pursuit of justice
is no virtue.*

*Barry Goldwater
U.S. Senator—Arizona*

HISTORY LESSONS

No great nation in history has ever remained great. Nations seem intent on committing suicide; no nation to date has withstood the cancerous decay of success over the ravages of time. Great nations' past successes and their pride blind them to the new realities they face; like all warrior generals, they refight the last war and constantly relive their days of glory—throughout their decline.

Americans in 1989 are consuming and spending more than we produce. We have gone from a creditor nation to a debtor nation. Our productivity rate has been on the decline for the last two decades.[2]

Paul Kennedy's book, *Rise and Fall of the Great Powers*[3], discusses how history and speculation using the enormous mass of data from the past can be used to study the development and decline of nations today. There exists a dynamic for change, driven chiefly by economic and technological developments, which then impacts upon social structures, political systems, military power, and the position of individual states and empires. Military power rests on adequate supplies of wealth, which, in turn, derive from a flourishing production base, healthy finances, and superior technology. All of the major shifts in the world's military power balances have followed alterations in the productive balances. And, further, the rising and falling of the various empires and states in the international system has been confirmed by the outcomes of the major power wars, where victory has always gone to the side with the greatest material resources.

1

The demand of most, if not all, governing bodies as we head into the twenty-first century is three-fold. First, the country has to provide military security for its national interests; second, the government has to satisfy the socioeconomic needs of its citizens; and third, government and industry have to ensure sustained economic, productivity growth. Without a rough balance between the competing demands of defense, consumption, and investment, a nation is unlikely to preserve its status as a great power.

THE QUALITY IMPERATIVE

During the Reagan-Bush legacy, the United States enjoyed the longest peacetime expansion in its history. Interest rates stabilized, unemployment reached its lowest level in 15 years, overall manufacturing output maintained its share of gross national product, and manufacturing productivity increased at a healthy pace.[4]

Yet, these overall strengths mask significant challenges in certain sectors of the overall U.S. economy: in particular, large-scale manufacturing. Many U.S. industries are battling aggressive and innovative competitors. The steel, apparel, textile, automobile, consumer electronics, and telecommunications industries, among others, have taken heavy blows from heavyweight foreign contenders. Now the thrust seems to be moving into the aerospace and high technology areas. Perhaps the central new factor in our domestic life and work is the existence of a new global economic competition.

For the United States to remain strong, to grow, and to regain lost markets, we must recognize our weaknesses. A significant portion of our current trade deficit is due to the ability of foreign competitors to deliver higher quality products that either are novel, less costly to produce, promise better service, or offer some combination of these traits. The competitors—most notably the Japanese and the Pacific Rim nations—are challenging us now, not so much with better science or technology, but in the way they organize their work . . . in the way their firms and factories are organized and managed. The United States is being challenged through the commitment of these countries to the total quality concept.

What makes quality different from other competitiveness solutions is its emphasis on actually improving this nation's ability to compete in the world markets. Most of our solutions to date seek to relieve competitive pressures rather than strengthening our competitiveness. The many avenues currently pursued to streamline regulations, to ensure foreign market access, erect tariff barriers, etc., are all laudable efforts; however, they will be fruitless if "Made in the USA" is viewed as synonymous for costly and inferior products and services. Without a total commitment to quality, no amount of playing field "leveling" will obtain U.S. market share in fields that are on the technological cutting edge.

Total quality management (TQM) is a new management philosophy. In June 1987, *Business Week* noted ". . . Managing for quality means nothing less than a sweeping overhaul in corporate culture, a radical shift in management philosophy, and a permanent commitment at all levels of the organization to seek continuous improvement."[5]

QUEST FOR EXCELLENCE—TOTAL QUALITY MANAGEMENT

Quality experts estimate that the total cost of poor quality, or the cost of not doing the right things right the first time, is approximately 20% of gross sales for manufacturing companies and 30% for service industries. Total U.S. production of goods and services is an estimated $3.7 trillion—so the quality "target," the potential "savings" from TQM, is a staggering $920 billion that can be saved or redirected for better use. These wastes and inefficiencies hurt business on the margin, and it's on the margin that they rise and fall. . . . It's on the margin that nations rise and fall.[4]

The TQM concept is now used in Japan and in some U.S. companies. This TQM thrust, however, must be used in the Department of Defense (DoD) and in all U.S. businesses—to avoid waste in all forms. Studies have shown that 95% of the effort in producing a product is consumed by activities other than the physical act of making it.[6] In the past, the primary focus has been on that physical 5% and almost no attention paid to the remaining 95%. The DoD, along with industry and the U.S. Congress, must now declare war on these potentially inefficient and costly priorities. The journey to TQM is an ambitious one; it means protection of the Free World, and there is no room for failure.

Effecting Change

Four problems are anticipated in effecting change.

- Impatience—We all have a predilection for quick fixes, a need to see immediate results. But as Secretary of Defense Cheney has said, there is no silver bullet for success. Reform will be a long, slow, arduous process.

Figure 1-1   THE CORPORATE MANAGEMENT STYLE CYCLE

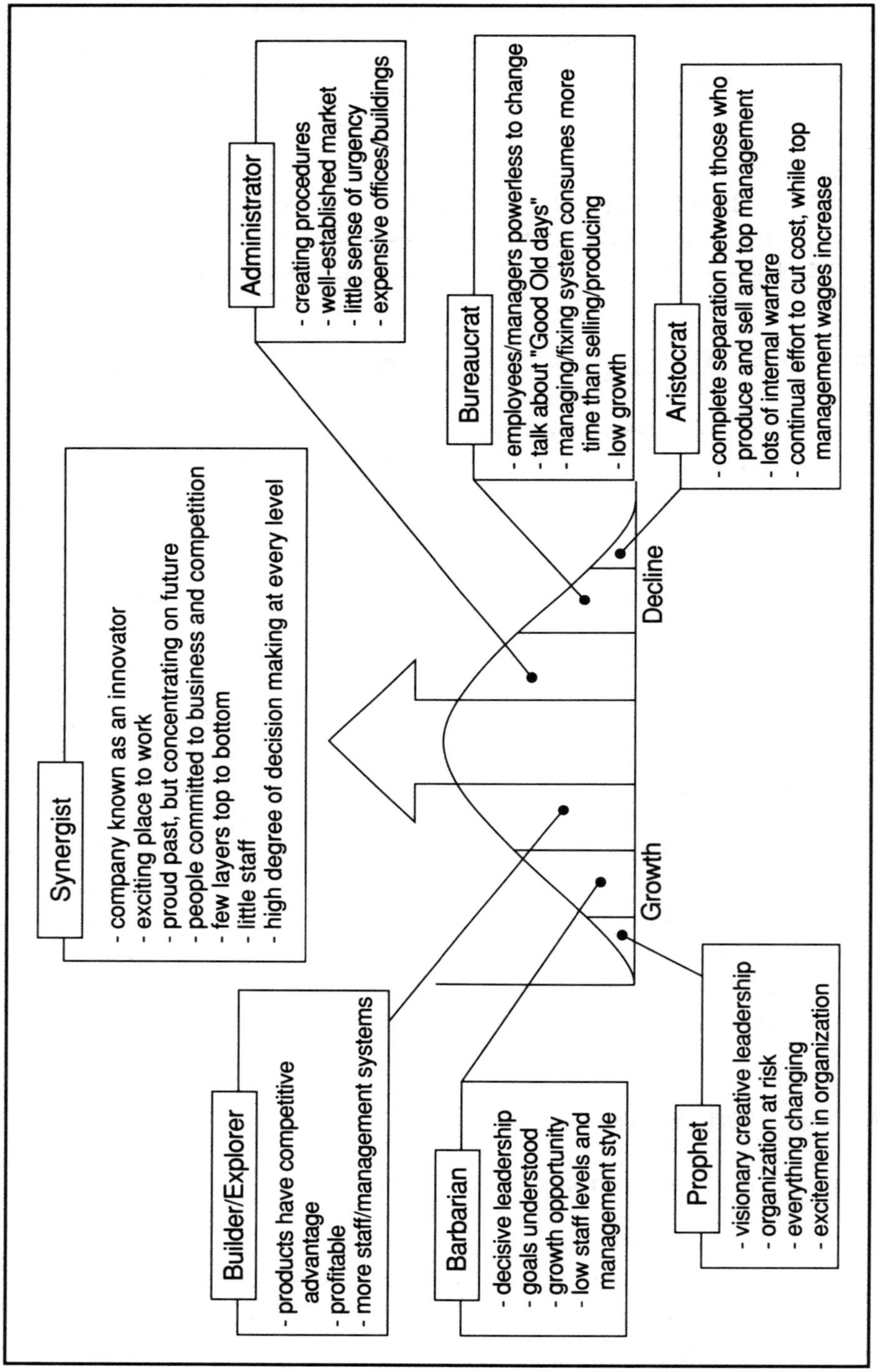

Administrator

- creating procedures
- well-established market
- little sense of urgency
- expensive offices/buildings

Bureaucrat

- employees/managers powerless to change
- talk about "Good Old days"
- managing/fixing system consumes more time than selling/producing
- low growth

Aristocrat

- complete separation between those who produce and sell and top management
- lots of internal warfare
- continual effort to cut cost, while top management wages increase

Synergist

- company known as an innovator
- exciting place to work
- proud past, but concentrating on future
- people committed to business and competition
- few layers top to bottom
- little staff
- high degree of decision making at every level

Builder/Explorer

- products have competitive advantage
- profitable
- more staff/management systems

Barbarian

- decisive leadership
- goals understood
- growth opportunity
- low staff levels and management style

Prophet

- visionary creative leadership
- organization at risk
- everything changing
- excitement in organization

Decline

Growth

Source: *Barbarians to Bureaucrats*, Lawrence M. Miller (8).

- Resistance—Defenders of the status quo are always threatened by the prospect of change. It will take consistency, constancy of purpose, tenacity, and perseverance to bring about the needed reforms.

- Parochialism—Everyone who has a stake in the process—DoD, Congress, and industry—must all be committed to optimizing the overall process, even when a specific solution may not be optimum from their particular viewpoint.

- Superficiality—We must differentiate between treating the symptoms and treating the root causes. Above all, we must be careful not to mistake activity for accomplishment.

"We are mired in a crazy quilt of rules, procedures, regulations, and laws that go a long way toward making it difficult, if not impossible, for the men and women in government and industry who have to make the process work—to make it work."[7]

SUMMARY

Our nation and our corporations have to change their styles to compete internally in U.S. markets and externally in world markets. The corporate cycle has to evolve from an aristocratic management style through synergism to the barbarian/prophet style of management (Figure 1–1).[8]

The resounding answer to the question, "Should we change?" has to be a **thundering yes!**

Management—Theories, Techniques, Gurus

2

*Experience is a hard teacher
because she gives the test first,
the lesson afterwards.*

Vernon Law

Is work a punishment, or does it depend on the conditions? Are Japanese management techniques the way to go? Or, are we having industry and national problems because of unsound management practices, policies, and theories? The answer—from my own experiences and after reading many different books and magazine articles, participating in countless seminars, and listening to hundreds of speakers—is that we fail because we cannot master people or manipulate them, or because we ignore the people who work with us and for us. Our challenge today is to shift from managers who tell workers what to do, to managers who act as facilitators and developers of the human potential. The ideal manager will have to use a combination of all theories and practices available to fit the existing solution(s).

THEORIES—COMPARING X, Y, AND Z

Two especially interesting management theorists are Douglas McGregor (Theory X and Y) and William Ouichi (Theory Z). Theories X and Y were postulated in the 1950s and Theory Z was defined in 1981.[9]

Theory X

Theory X was adapted from two effective examples of management techniques for providing control of a particular population: the military and the Catholic church. These organizations have extensive control of their members through a system of punishments. The ultimate punishment in the military is death; in the church it is excommunication (the symbolic equivalent of death). Of course, such severe punishments are not socially acceptable in a modern industrial environment. Theory X, which depends to a great extent on punishment for controlling the work force, is thus an ineffective management technique in most situations.

Theory X is based on three precepts:

1. The average human being has an inherent dislike of work and will avoid it if possible.

2. Because of the human characteristic of disliking work, most people must be coerced, controlled, directed, and threatened with punishment to get them to put forth adequate effort toward the achievement of organizational objectives.

3. The average human being prefers to be directed, wishes to avoid responsibility, has relatively little ambition, and wants security above all.

One of McGregor's most interesting observations of the reasons why Theory X practitioners fail to achieve a successful and efficient organization is that the rewards (wages, fringe benefits, vacations, profit sharing, etc.) can be used to satisfy people's needs only when they leave their jobs. Thus, work is perceived as a form of punishment, the price to be paid for obtaining various kinds of satisfaction away from the job.

Theory Y

McGregor also proposed Theory Y, based on the following precepts:

1. The expenditure of physical and mental effort in work is as natural as play or rest. The average human being does not inherently dislike work. Depending upon controllable conditions, work may be a source of satisfaction (and will be voluntarily performed) or a source of punishment (and will be avoided if possible).

2. External control and the threat of punishment are not the only means for bringing about effort toward organizational objectives. People will exercise self-direction and self-control in the service of objectives to which they are committed.

3. Commitment to objectives is a function of the rewards associated with their achievement. The most significant of such rewards, e.g., the satisfaction of ego and self-actualization needs, can be direct products of effort directed toward organizational objectives.

4. The average human being learns, under proper conditions, not only to accept but to seek responsibility. Avoidance of responsibility, lack of ambition, and emphasis on security are generally consequences of experience, not inherent human characteristics.

5. The capacity to exercise a relatively high degree of imagination, ingenuity, and creativity in the solution of organizational problems is widely, not narrowly, distributed in the population.

6. Under the conditions of modern industrial life, the intellectual potentialities of the average human being are only partially utilized.

Theory Y requires selective adaptation rather than a single absolute form of control and recognizes people as resources with substantial potential rather than uninspired hands. Theory Y also requires managerial effort to integrate the personal needs and goals of the worker with those of the organization. It is not sufficient to issue orders and fire anyone who does not conform.

Theory Z

Much has been said of the effectiveness of Japanese management techniques. William Ouichi made an extensive study of a number of major Japanese corporations as well as a large number of American corporations. Based on these observations, he formulated Theory Z, which essentially describes the policies of a number of successful American corporations, modified somewhat to account for his observations in Japan.[9]

Characteristics of the Japanese industrial society include:

1. About 35% of the Japanese work force is committed to lifetime employment (in large industries and government bureaus). The Japanese use female employees as the temporary work force. Industry compensates for peaks and valleys in the work load by altering the size of the annual bonuses, by shifting workers between jobs, and by expanding and shrinking their subcontract work. Pirating of personnel is nonexistent. As a result, workers have only one goal—to prosper as their company prospers.

2. For the first 10 years, all employees are treated the same with respect to salary and promotions. During this period, the employees learn all facets of company operation by rotating from

one small group to another. Peer pressure ensures that they contribute to the output of each group. Formal evaluation of an employee's ability does not start until after the 10-year indoctrination and evaluation period. Those selected for advancement or salary increases know every aspect of the operation, and are known by most of the work force.

3. Job rotation continues throughout a person's career. This further enhances the spirit of cooperation between employees, and broadens the viewpoints of the managers.

4. Corporate decision making is reached by consensus. Since all participants have an intimate knowledge of all facets of the operation, and career advancement procedures preclude short-term personal goals, the decisions reached are usually those that are best for the organization.

5. The Japanese workers accept and believe in collectivism. All activities are viewed as a team effort, performed by equals.

6. Japanese industries are concerned about the well-being of the family as well as the individual. A great deal of effort is devoted to ensuring that the family is included in recreation and other corporate activities. Companies feel responsible to the families for the proper training, indoctrination, and moral supervision of young employees.

With this background in the Japanese way of life and of doing business, Ouichi then reviewed a number of American companies. He found that many of the most consistently successful companies exhibited a number of traits similar to their Japanese counterparts. He named these companies *Theory Z companies*.

Ouichi has identified and defined in detail 13 steps necessary to transform an organization into a Theory Z organization. These steps are:

1. Understand the Theory Z philosophy.

2. Audit the company's existing philosophy.

3. Define an appropriate management philosophy.

4. Implement this new philosophy.

5. Develop interpersonal skills.

6. Evaluate progress.

7. Involve the union.

8. Stabilize employment.

9. Develop a system for slow evaluation and promotion.

10. Broaden career path development.

11. Implement programs at the lowest level.

12. Seek areas of improvement.

13. Develop holistic relationships.

It will be noted that Steps 1 through 10 are oriented toward developing management attitudes. The Theory Z organization will be successful only if fully supported by all levels of management.

Many Theory Z organizations have written corporate philosophies that define, in broad terms, an intent to treat customers fairly, to treat employees fairly, to produce a quality product, and to operate the business in a manner intended to foster long-term growth.

BUSINESS TECHNIQUES

There are a lot of techniques to solve problems, get people involved, and handle unusual situations. Executives, however, should not latch on to management techniques that look like a quick fix. There's nothing inherently wrong with any of these ideas. What's wrong is that too many companies use them as gimmicks to evade the basic challenges they face. Unless such solutions are well thought out, integrated into a process such as TQM, and supported by a sincere, involved commitment from top management, they are doomed to fail. They quickly become meaningless buzz words, hollow symbols, mere fads; and senior management becomes a laughing symbol from below!

Business Week summarized some of the techniques utilized during the past four decades in an article entitled "Business Fads: What's In—and Out."[10] Let's explore all these wonderful concepts that work, if used appropriately.

The 1950s

- Computerization—The first corporate mainframes were displayed as symbols of progress.

- Theory Y—As propounded by MIT Professor Douglas McGregor, this philosophy held that people produce more if they have a say in their work.

- Quantitative Management—Trust the numbers, running a business is a science, not an art.
- Diversification—The strategy of countering cyclical ups and downs by buying other businesses.
- Management by Objectives—Peter Drucker popularized the process of setting an executive's goals through negotiation.

The 1960s

- T-Groups—Encounter seminars for managers, designed to teach them interpersonal sensitivity.
- Centralization/Decentralization—One school says that headquarters should make the decisions; the other places responsibility in the hands of line managers.
- Matrix Management—A system by which a manager may report to different superiors according to task.
- Conglomeration—Putting disparate businesses under a single corporate umbrella.
- The Managerial Grid—A method of determining whether a manager's chief concern is people or production.

The 1970s

- Zero-Based Budgeting—Throw out last year's numbers and start from scratch when making up this year's budget.
- The Experience Curve—Generating profits by cutting prices, increasing market share, and boosting efficiency.
- Portfolio Management—A ranking system that identifies some businesses as cash cows, some as stars, and some as dogs.

The 1980s

- Theory Z—Proponents of Japanese management methods argue that U.S. companies should adopt such management techniques as quality circles and job enrichment.
- Entrepreneuring—Encouraging executives to create and control entrepreneurial projects throughout the corporation.
- Demassing—A popular euphemism for trimming the work force and demoting managers.

Figure 2-1   COMMON THREADS AMONG MANAGEMENT PHILOSOPHIES

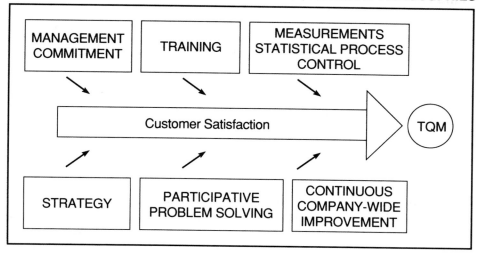

- Restructuring—Sweeping out businesses that don't measure up, often while taking on considerable debt. Wall Street usually applauds these moves.

- Corporate Culture—The values, goals, rituals, and heroes that characterize a company's style.

- One-Minute Managing—Balancing praise and reproach in 60 seconds.

- Management by Walking Around—Leaving the office to visit the troops instead of relying on written reports.

QUALITY GURUS

In developing a total quality management culture, there are different roads to follow, different techniques—discussed previously—to be used; but the roads **all** can lead to the same renaissance. When attempting to find the best route, an approach often begins with an expert, a consultant, or a *guru*. The concepts of three noted quality gurus—Crosby, Deming, and Juran—provide road maps to establish a quality culture. Although the routes they suggest differ somewhat, their destination can be world-class quality.[11]

Company-wide total quality generally involves several major ingredients. Figure 2–1 represents the common threads of the three gurus.

Management Commitment

Each expert begins by emphasizing management commitment. Crosby has it as the first item in his 14-step process (Figure 2–2). Dr. Deming addresses all 14 points to management, but Point 14 clearly addresses the permanent commitment to quality (Figure 2–3). Similarly, Dr. Juran urges all management levels to provide leadership by taking on their own quality projects in the "Journey from Symptom to Cause" (Figure 2–4).

Strategy

There has to be structure and strategy in the journey to quality improvement. Crosby established a quality improvement team in Step 2 to run the process and change the attitude and culture throughout the total organization; e.g., the zero defects day. Dr. Deming's theme is to create a top management structure to push all 14 points. Dr. Juran recommends that a steering council guide the process and track improvements project-by-project with emphasis on the cost of quality.

Training

All three emphasize training, but with slightly different focuses. Crosby's training is targeted toward developing a new culture and implementing the *quality improvement program* (QIP). Deming's focus is on

Figure 2-2 CROSBY'S QUALITY PROCESS

1. Management
2. Quality improvement team
3. Quality measurement
4. Cost of quality evaluation
5. Awareness
6. Corrective action
7. Zero defects planning
8. Quality education
9. Zero defects day
10. Goal setting
11. Error cause removal
12. Recognition
13. Quality councils
14. Do it all over again

Figure 2-3   DR. W. EDWARDS DEMING'S 14 POINTS

1. CREATE CONSTANCY OF PURPOSE FOR IMPROVEMENT OF PRODUCT AND SERVICE
2. ADOPT THE NEW PHILOSOPHY OF REFUSING TO ALLOW DEFECTS
3. CEASE DEPENDENCE ON MASS INSPECTION AND RELY ONLY ON STATISTICAL CONTROL
4. REQUIRE SUPPLIERS TO PROVIDE STATISTICAL EVIDENCE OF QUALITY
5. CONSTANTLY AND FOREVER IMPROVE PRODUCTION AND SERVICE
6. TRAIN ALL EMPLOYEES
7. GIVE ALL EMPLOYEES THE PROPER TOOLS TO DO THE JOB RIGHT
8. ENCOURAGE COMMUNICATION AND PRODUCTIVITY
9. ENCOURAGE DIFFERENT DEPARTMENTS TO WORK TOGETHER ON PROBLEM SOLVING
10. ELIMINATE POSTERS AND SLOGANS THAT DO NOT TEACH SPECIFIC IMPROVEMENT METHODS
11. USE STATISTICAL METHODS TO CONTINUOUSLY IMPROVE QUALITY AND PRODUCTIVITY
12. ELIMINATE ALL BARRIERS TO PRIDE IN WORKMANSHIP
13. PROVIDE ONGOING RETRAINING TO KEEP PACE WITH CHANGING PRODUCTS, METHODS, ETC.
14. CLEARLY DEFINE TOP MANAGEMENT'S PERMANENT COMMITMENT TO QUALITY

statistical techniques. Juran covers quality management practices and problem-solving techniques; he provides a systems approach to QIP and improvement for all parts of the organization.

People Involvement and Rewards

One of the most important milestones on the journey to a QIP is removing sources of problems. Step 11 of Crosby's process focuses on removing the causes of errors. That step, plus his emphasis on conformance to requirements, helps address the category of problems that Dr. Juran calls the "trivial many." Drs. Deming and Juran both maintain that 85% of the problems are management controllable, not worker controllable. Dr. Deming uses statistical process control (SPC) to separate common versus special sources. Dr. Juran also urges management to address both chronic and sporadic problems. Dr. Juran

Figure 2-4   J.M. JURAN'S JOURNEY FROM SYMPTOM TO CAUSE

QUALITY IMPROVEMENT IN ACTION

	ACTIVITIES	STEERING ARM	DIAGNOSTIC ARM
	ASSIGN PRIORITY TO PROJECTS	x	
	PARETO ANALYSIS OF SYMPTOMS		x
	THEROIZE ON CAUSE OF SYMPTOMS	x	
JOURNEY FROM SYMPTOM TO CAUSE	TEST THEORIES; COLLECT, ANALYZE DATA		x
	NARROW LIST OF THEORIES	x	
	DESIGN EXPERIMENT(S)		x
	APPROVE DESIGN; PROVIDE AUTHORITY	x	
	CONDUCT EXPERIMENTS; ESTBALISH PROOF OF CAUSE		x
JOURNEY FROM CAUSE TO REMEDY	PROPOSE REMEDIES	x	
	TEST REMEDY		x
	ACTION TO INSTITUTE REMEDY		
	CONTROL NEW LEVEL		

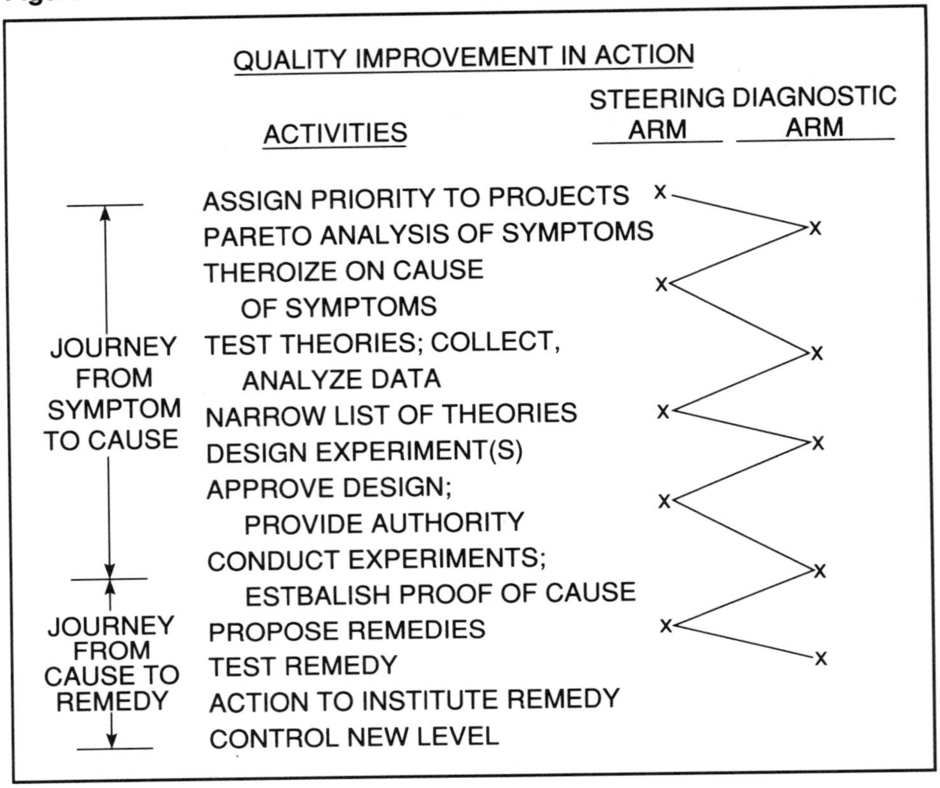

provides the how-tos in helping operators achieve Crosby's performance standard of zero defects.

Quality Measurement

Crosby, Deming, and Juran all recognize the importance of measurement to track progress and ensure that the plan(s) stay on course. Although they all promote direct measures of performance, such as assembly line defects or engineering drawing errors, Deming places more emphasis on statistical analysis. The three gurus provide different directions regarding the cost of quality (or *un*quality). Crosby and Juran both view the cost of quality as the main QIP measurement when selecting quality improvement projects. Deming opposes the cost of quality as a measurement because it does not address the largest factor: customer dissatisfaction.

The belief in a need for a cost of quality measurement is in direct proportion to the belief of top management that "quality is not free" and so desires a cost measurement for the QIP projects. Top managements' language is dollars. Its question is always: What is the return of investment? The TQM advocate has to be able to relate what the waste or non-value added things are, where they are, and how this information can be used to improve the process. Nearly all companies need to develop a cost of quality system that addresses the total organization from marketing/sales to field service. Direct measures, cost of quality, and statistical data are all required, but will receive different emphasis by different parts of the organization. We will discuss a model for the cost of unquality in Chapter 6.

Continuous Improvement

Crosby, Deming, and Juran all preach the need for initiating a culture of continuous improvement. Crosby urges setting goals, going through the process, and then going back to Step 1 and doing it again and again. Dr. Juran urges management to create an annual QIP with goals and specific projects—his approach fits in best with management by objectives (MBOs). Dr. Deming also emphasizes ongoing improvement by Step 5 and the Deming circle. The circle process is plan-do-check-analyze-act.

TQM

Total quality management utilizes a combination of all the methods from the theories, techniques, and quality gurus as discussed in this chapter—and all of them can be used for achieving world-class quality. In establishing TQM, a company should fit the applicable pieces of any or all of these methods into its strategy for changing the culture. A company can tailor a quality strategy based on these ideologies and avoid the conflict involved with trying to choose a proper champion or guru. Only by creating its own "route" will a company have the greatest chance of developing a sound strategy for economic survival.

CASE STUDY—BOEING COMMERCIAL AIRPLANE COMPANY

Boeing launched its continuous quality improvement process in late 1984. The company president, Dean D. Thornton, established a Quality Improvement Center (QIC) in Seattle, Washington. It was staffed with people from throughout the company—a group of resident experts to do the training, coordination, and monitoring of the projects and total process. Their strategy is depicted in Figure 2–5.

**Figure 2-5   BOEING'S CONTINUOUS QUALITY
IMPROVEMENT STRATEGY**

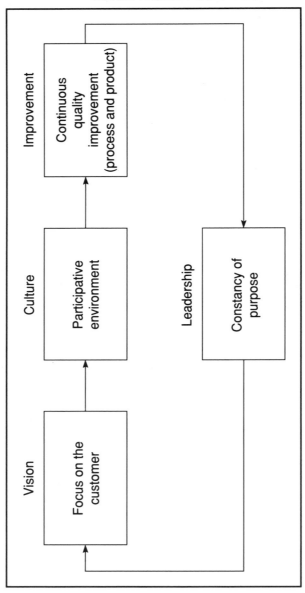

After they assembled a small QIC staff, they visited companies that were benchmarks of the improvement process centers of excellence. These were ARMCO, Ford Motor Company, Hewlett-Packard, Honeywell Aerospace and Defense, IBM, McDonnell-Douglas Electronics Company, Motorola, and Tektronix. They then selected the gurus to assist them in their journey. The gurus that were used, either in residence or through their materials, were the Reiker Management Systems, W. Edwards Deming, William E. Conway, J. M. Juran, and Philip B. Crosby.

Boeing's current improvement process is shown in Figure 2–6. To summarize, this is top management leadership, the vision of customers and people focuses, which drives the business strategies and finally focuses the business process. The business process analysis is a method for analyzing how work is accomplished to identify areas of improvement. A high-quality process is identified as having the following characteristics:

- Effective—Achieves the intended results, meeting the customer's requirements.

- Efficient—Operates with minimum resources.

- Under control—Tasks are documented, responsibilities are clearly defined, variability is minimal.

- Monitored—Key control indicators are in use to identify changes in the process. (Note: Indicators are specifically covered in Chapter 5. Although the author's list is not all inclusive, it provides the thought process of possibilities.)

- Value-added—Contribution to business is defined, measured, and tracked. (Note: A conceptual quality cost model is covered in Chapter 6; again the author's model is not all inclusive, but it is a viable model.)

Boeing then began its "Stairway of Training." The QIC conducts training seminars and teaches the concepts, techniques, and tools of continuous quality improvement as depicted in Figure 2–7. [The author also lectured at Boeing in May 1986 on the quality improvement program in place since 1982 at General Dynamics, and is using material that was provided during the two-day seminar.[12] Boeing and GD have shared insights into the process during trade-off visits to each company's facilities. Under the USAF Advanced Tactical Fighter program, this sharing continues with the Lockheed, Boeing, and General Dynamics contracting team concept.]

Boeing is aggressively moving out with their Quality Improvement Center process. Members of the Boeing QIC visited General Dynamics in the fall of 1989 and again shared the progress being made as shown in Figure 2–8. At that time, three of their total quality asso-

Figure 2-6 BOEING'S CONTINUOUS QUALITY IMPROVEMENT PROCESS

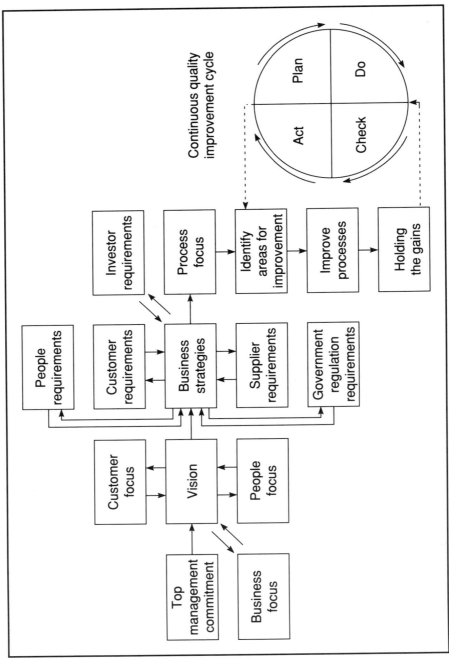

Figure 2-7   BOEING'S STAIRWAY OF TRAINING

Business process improvement

Design of experiments

Process improvement workshop

Process control methods

Introduction to process control

Team member

Facilitator

Team leader

Managing quality seminar

Leadership seminar

ciates also analyzed General Dynamics' TQM process, and its data and measurement systems.

Boeing's QIC system is heavily rooted in the Juran, Deming, Myron Tribus, Conway, Taguchi, and Crosby philosophies as depicted through videos, books, and lectures. Their system is achieving success similar to that of other companies who have embarked on the TQM journey. For specifics, their QIC personnel can be contacted for your own company's benchmarking start to TQM.*

SUMMARY

Running any business is both an art and a science, but it is not a game of quick-fixing by fads. There is much merit in the fact that a corporation's culture—its shared values, beliefs, and rituals—strongly influence its failure or success. But a culture is built over years, not overnight. The management of total quality requires a complete and comprehensive look at all these business fads as tools to be integrated into a strategy or game plan. Motorola, Honeywell, and Boeing Commercial Aircraft have done just that. They have adopted TQM as the

---

*Boeing Commercial Aircraft, Quality Improvement Center, P.O. Box 3707, MIS 6P-40, Seattle, WA 98124–2207.

Figure 2-8   BOEING'S QUALITY IMPROVEMENT CENTER HISTORY

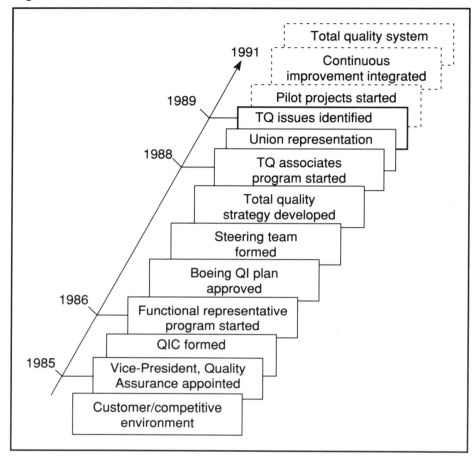

philosophical strategy, formed a central training group, and are slowly changing their culture. Motorola recently won the U.S. Malcolm Baldridge National Quality Award for their Six-Sigma process; Boeing has a business backlog that is the envy of the aerospace industry, and they are charging in the world marketplace.

And all of us are searching for excellence. The march continues—will TQM provide a solution? National policies, quality excellence, and targeted industries have made Japan the world's economic power, let's regain our heritage with total quality management.

Strategy "2000"

3

It takes real talent to withstand adversity,
but it takes genius to survive success.

Samuel Rutgers
17th Century

EXISTENCE IN YEAR 2000

Predictions are that 40% of the manufacturing jobs in the United States will be reduced by the year 2000.[13] Lester Thurow, Dean of the Business School at MIT says the U.S. economic condition is at its weakest since World War II. Jack Grayson, Chairman of the American Productivity and Quality Center, suggests that our nation has less than two decades to improve quality and productivity in order to maintain the economic strength enjoyed during this past century.[14]

STRATEGIC PLANNING

Does your company have a strategic plan? Does it address quality and productivity, or does it only address marketing, finances, and capitalization? Developing an overall strategy for improving quality and productivity that will be accepted and effectively implemented is an important and challenging task.

There are a number of strategies and techniques for improvement (some were covered in Chapter 2), but proper selection, integration, and implementation of these strategies and techniques are the keys to long-term improvement and economic survival. The key thrust here is to define TQM performance measurements and provide one real-life model for the *cost of unquality*. Measurements indicate whether we are doing the necessary things laid out in our planning and whether we are being successful. If there is to be true TQM with continuous improvement, measurements are a must.

The competitive world we are in requires that we not only embrace the philosophy of constant and continuous improvement, but we must make the philosophy operational—not just another fad! The challenge of gaining excellence forces us to reexamine our vision, QIP, and other improvement strategies—as well as our theories, our techniques, and our standards of excellence.

PLANNING MODEL

The DoD funded a six-year study on a guidance document relative to quality and productivity management. The model (Figure 3–1) described in the study, and process is currently in use at Honeywell Aerospace and Defense, among others. The model and process is contained in a manual published by the Defense Systems Management College.[14]

Step 1—Organizational Systems Analysis

The first step in the planning process is designed to prepare the management team to plan. *Organizational systems analysis (OSA)* involves eight basic areas of analysis and is designed to be accomplished in a structured, participative fashion by a management team (Figure 3–1). The eight areas of analysis are:

1. Vision (corporate long-range objectives).
2. Guiding principles (values and beliefs).
3. Mission (purpose).
4. Input/output analysis.
5. Internal strategic analysis.
6. External strategic analysis.
7. Current performance levels.
8. Roadblocks to performance improvement.

Answers to the inevitable questions raised by OSA may already exist, but they may not have been effectively communicated or may need to be reviewed and clarified. Procedures can be developed to assist with the process of data collection.

Figure 3-1   PLANNING MODEL

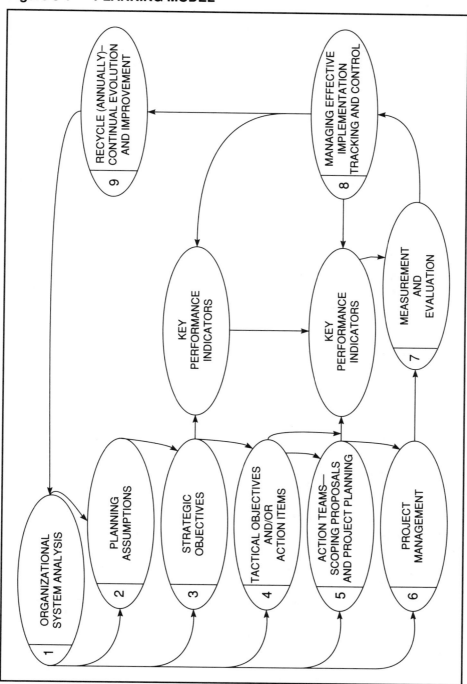

(Source: Sink and Tuttle, 1989)

Step 2—Planning Assumptions

Step 2 converts the data shared in Step 1 into specific planning assumptions. Assumptions can have a dramatic influence on what must be considered while developing the plan and must be clearly understood by everyone. The desired outcome of Step 2 is an awareness and group consensus as to the importance and validity of the various planning assumptions. The process for accomplishing this is:

1. The planning team members each silently generate a list of assumptions.

2. A round-robin process is used to solicit the list of assumptions. The assumptions are written on flip-chart paper and taped to room walls. Each assumption is numbered sequentially in the order in which it is listed on the flip-chart paper. Lists of 30 to 60 assumptions are not uncommon.

3. Each team member is then given an importance-validity grid. The number of each assumption is then put in the square that best describes how critical and certain it is.

4. All the grids are collected, and one grid for each assumption is then created.

5. Analysis and discussion of the assumptions follow.

Step 3—Strategic Objectives

The question being addressed in Step 3 is: What must we, as an organization, accomplish in the next "x" years? (A typical planning horizon is five to seven years.)

A proven efficient and effective technique for executing Step 3 is the nominal group technique (NGT). The NGT process increases commitment to the final plan, improves communication and coordination, and leads to effective implementation. The resulting set of objectives is audited against the output from Steps 1 and 2 to ensure consistency. Step 3 takes about two-and-a-half hours for the initial cut. The output from the NGT session will have to be revised and clarified to present **upline** to upper management or to different audiences within your organization.

The issue of measurement often arises at this point. *Key performance indicators* (KPIs) should be developed for each objective. KPIs address the following questions:

- Have we met our objective? (an effectiveness issue)

- Were resources consumed wisely? (an efficiency issue)

- Have we met our quality standards?
- What will be the impact on performance?

Step 4—Action Items

Using the previously generated strategic objectives as a guide, a series of action items needs to be developed. Step 4 is identical to Step 3 with respect to how it is accomplished. Two things change, however. First, Step 4 deals with start, not finish, issues. Second, the planning period shifts from five to seven years to zero to three years.

There are also two traps to avoid in Step 4, that is *start versus finish* and *must versus want*. First, the objectives identified in Step 3 involve finish, not start, issues. The objectives identified are those you must or want to complete at or before the end of the stated planning period. Second, you should differentiate between *must* objectives and *want* objectives. You have only limited discretionary time and resources; making everything a must objective will paralyze the organization and the planning effort. You should only use the voting and ranking step of the NGT for want, not must, objectives.

Step 5—Action Teams

Step 5 is the link between planning and effective implementation. Volunteer teams of three to five people are identified to develop scoping proposals. These teams are the managers involved in Steps 1–4 and may be supplemented by staff and lower level managers and employees. These teams are given approximately one month to develop a scoping proposal for their respective action items. A scoping proposal addresses such things as:

- What has to be done?
- Who has to be involved?
- When should activities occur?
- How should the project be implemented?
- What are the associated costs and benefits?
- What are the measures of success?

A completed scoping proposal should be fewer than five pages in length and should "scope out" implementation planning. Many organizations incorporate a review and evaluation process in this step. Scoping proposals are reviewed by a quality and productivity council or committee composed of members of the planning team. Once a "green light" is given to each scoping proposal, an implementation team is formed.

The elapsed time from Step 1 to the completion of Step 5 should be no longer than three months and should precede setting a budget by three to four months so that the plan drives the budget, not the reverse.

Again there are traps to avoid in this step. Be sure that no one is on more than one action team. The planning process has a tendency to get people "fired up" and causes them to volunteer for more than they are able to do. Don't assign people to action items no one volunteered to tackle. Remember, not everything needs to be done today!

Step 6—Project Management

Project management is both a science and an art. However, the art, the skill, and the discipline associated with this step of performance improvement planning are far more important than any specific project management technique. Effective project management, as experienced managers know, requires attention to detail, persistence, impatience, patience, consistency, discipline, communication, and coordination, as well as the application of appropriate techniques.

Step 7—Measurement and Evaluation

Step 7 of the planning process involves measuring, assessing, and evaluating the impact of strategic and tactical objectives on organizational system performance. Planning team members are held accountable for tracking implementation progress and for measuring impacts using new or existing measures or measurement systems. Many organizations develop a visibility room for displaying these measures. This step continues for the duration of the year and provides data for repeating the process next year.

Step 8—Managing Effective Implementation

Continuous support from management and a visible tracking system will help ensure effective implementation. Having quarterly review meetings will help track progress: a half-day session for the first and third quarter reviews; a full-day session for the mid-year review; and a two- or three-day fourth quarter session to review progress, update the plan, and identify ways to improve the process.

Step 9—Recycle (Annually)—Continual Evolution and Development

It is essential for any company to tailor and modify this process annually. Involvement and participation in the process will vary from company to company, but the process can still be applied to a division on down to a work group, or even to a programmatic thrust; i.e., a quality and productivity effort.

CASE STUDY—GLOBE METALLURGICAL, INC.

Does planning and using TQM theories, techniques, and gurus work? Ask Globe Metallurgical, Inc., producers of ferro-alloys and silicon metal products. It has realized major improvements in quality, productivity, and cost from using these concepts. How is its performance?

- 380% increase in productivity in three years.
- $500,000 company income per employee per year.
- All suggestions answered in 24 hours.
- 40 to 1 return on the money invested in the improvement process.
- Returned products dropped from 44 lots to zero in two years.
- The average employee received a $5,000 profit-sharing bonus in 1988.
- Their share of the ductile iron market jumped from less than 5% to greater than 50% in three years.
- Upper management serves as facilitators in the quality training activities. Their type of employee orientation makes for an enthusiastic, challenged, informed, and proud work force and company. It has resulted in enhancement of the company's reputation by:
    - Winning the Malcolm Baldrige National Quality Award in 1988—the first small company to do so.
    - Being the first winner of the Shingu Prize for Manufacturing Excellence.

- Continuously setting new quality records for the Ford and GM supplier awards.

SUMMARY

The year 2000 will be here soon enough, and the planning has to, or needs to, start now. In putting together the strategic plan, the uppermost ingredient to remember is the quality of everything done. One model has been discussed, but there are others that can be utilized. What is important is to have a vision for the future, plan it, and implement it.

Meeting these challenges—the current state of government and industry relations, and preparing for the future—will require an entirely new vision. Our educational system demands enhancement. Our government/industry climate will need a new focus on the quality of processes and personnel. Innovative management practices are urgently needed to harness the valuable, declining human resources that are the prerequisite to change.

Journey to TQM 4

*There is nothing more wasteful
than doing efficiently that which is not necessary.*

Sir Royce

WHY?

A vision of TQM cannot be established in an organization by edict or coercion. It is more an act of persuasion, of creating an enthusiastic and dedicated commitment to that vision—as described in Chapter 3. Why? Because it is right for the times, for the organization, and right for the people working toward it.

STANDARDS OF SURVIVAL

The new competition is performing at impressive levels. Knowing who your competitors are and how good they are is simply good business sense. Numerous organizations are formalizing these processes and calling them *competitive benchmarking*. There is an excellent series of articles entitled "Benchmarking: The Search for Industry Best Practices That Lead to Superior Performance" in the February–June, 1989 *Quality Progress* magazine.

Studies have been done by the Defense Systems Management College comparing typical U.S. performance levels to the "new competition." Table 4–1 presents a summary of that study.[14]

The competitive challenge is a very intense race without a finish line. The increasing pace of opening world markets and more companies entering your business makes quality an important strategy. The planned strategy should be, let's start the journey to TQM.

Table 4-1   CHANGING STANDARDS OF SURVIVAL

Key Performance Indicators	Typical U.S. Performance Levels	Competition's Performance Levels
Quality	Parts per hundred Don't fix what isn't broken Reliance on inspection	Parts per thousand, ten thousand. . . Constant improvement Total quality management
Employee Involvement	Individual suggestion systems Employee involvement means anybody but management Win-lose/zero-sum games for sharing information, knowledge, power, and rewards One implemented improvement/employee/year	Team "proposal" systems Employee involvement means everybody in the organization Win-win/nonzero-sum games for sharing information, knowledge, power, and rewards 10, 20, 30, 40, or more implemented improvements/employee/year
Costs	Recover through customer price increases	Profitability through internal performance
Schedule	Financially driven	Quality and customer driven
Productivity	Through cost reduction and layoffs	Through increased quality, effectiveness, efficiency, quality of work life, innovation, customer orientation
Inventory System	Push "Just in case"	Pull "Just in time"
Technology and Innovation	Dedicated, complex, and sophisticated High-tech/low-touch "Technology will solve the problem" mentality	Appropriate and flexible, appropriately complex High-tech/high-touch Employees indicate where technology is needed most
Bottom line	Emphasis on operational plan, technical requirements of product Short-term profits, maintenance of the status quo	Emphasis on strategic plan Long-term growth, survival, competitiveness constant improvement

Source: Defense Systems Management College (14).

THE BASIC PROCESS

There are many theories, there are many techniques, and there are lots of gurus and consultants with their basic 14 points, their steps to quality improvement, etc. As defined by the Department of Defense, total quality management is a continuous quality improvement process that demands top management leadership and continuous involvement in the process activities.

What should a suggested model look like for the never-ending journey to TQM? The basics should include the steps from the TQM model shown in Figure 2–1 and some help from Dr. H. James Harrington in his article "A Guideline to Improvement."[15]

Top Management Commitment

The most important accomplishments within a company are the visions, pronouncements, and actions of the top executive. Although past efforts may have produced good results, the future holds that preeminence is needed for the future. One exemplary company (General Dynamics) has accepted the challenge and cranked up the competitive environment with leadership (Figure 4–1).

To achieve total organization involvement, top management must steer the quality improvement process towards excellence. A *steering committee* structure (Figure 4–2) with *critical process and corrective action teams* (Figure 4–3) is established. The critical process teams are formed by the steering committee to investigate high-level functional processes that have a critical impact on the company or division to satisfy customer requirements. Corrective action teams are then formed to address and formulate the "fixes" needed to improve pieces of the process(es) that have been identified and investigated by the critical process teams.

Strategy

Developing an overall strategy for TQM is an important and challenging task. Perhaps now is the time to select the guru for the TQM journey. The guru can then take the first trained, the top management staff, through a planning routine. These planning steps are (a) to develop a vision, (b) to define the mission, and (c) to postulate the strategic objectives and key performance indicators. Vision statements are hard to develop through consensus and may appear simplistic, but they are powerful requirements for the employees of the company, for the community, and for the customers. A vision might be:

Figure 4-1   TOTAL QUALITY MANAGEMENT

GENERAL DYNAMICS
Fort Worth DIvision

DIVISION NOTICE NO. 88-46

3 November 1988
To: All Supervision
Subject: Total Quality Management

The current national and corporate fiscal environment is such that the long—term viability of our division is dependent on providing our products and services at lowest total cost. A way of achieving that objective is to improve the quality of everything we do in the division. This will allow us to be more competitive and maintain and improve the favorable position we have.

Our customer is committed to a program of total quality. A Frank Carlucci, Secretary of Defense, states, "It is critical at this time that the department of defense; its contractors, and its vendors focus on "Quality as the vehicle for achieving higher levels of performance. The DoD budget leaves no room for solving problems that flow from poor quality."

In order to improve our products and our services, I am instituting a Total Quality Management (TQM) initiative. The objective is to prevent rather than detect and correct errors in every employee's work. TQM will provide a cohesion for instituting continuous quality management in the division. I expect all levels of division management to foster an environment which encourages and rewards involvement of all employees in this process. We are not changing our thrust from technical excellence but rather we expect to maintain that excellence and add to our current philosophy and way of thinking. We must manage people in addition to managing things. To do that we must establish an environment of trust and assign responsibility and authority at the lowest practical level. We must establish a means of ferreting out and solving systematic problems, and this can only be done by involving all of our employees in this process. It is the responsibility of all levels of Division Management to assure that those reporting to you are provided the proper resources to perform their assigned tasks, and that you and your people increase the level of team work and problem solving feedback with those people in your own and other departments.

I have requested the Resources Management department to be the division focal point for TQM activities. However, to accomplish the objectives outlined above will require the complete involvement of all employees at the Fort Worth Division. Your participation and involvement is absolutely essential if we are to succeed in this very important new direction for our division.

Charles A. Anderson
Vice President & General Manager

Figure 4-2   GENERAL DYNAMICS TQM STEERING COMMITTEE

RESEARCH & ENGINEERING VP
LOGISTICS VP
QUALITY ASSURANCE VP
MATERIAL VP
PRODUCTION VP
HUMAN RESOURCES VP
FINANCE VP
MARKETING VP
TQM OFFFICE–SECRETARY

•CHAIRMAN SELECTED BY COMMITTEE
•CHAIRMAN & SECRETARY BRIEF VP AND PRESIDENT ON ACTIONS AND DECISIONS

We are the Ocean Water Company. We provide high-technology chemicals for maintenance of an environmentally clean world. This is achieved through a caring partnership of:

> employees,
> community,
> suppliers,
> and customers.

A company or division mission could be:

> To produce the highest quality products at the lowest market cost through total employee involvement.

**Figure 4-3   GENERAL DYNAMICS TOTAL
ORGANIZATION INVOLVEMENT**

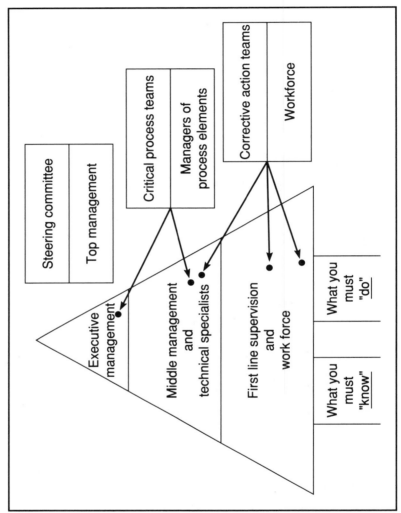

Next in the process of strategy is development of the strategic and tactical objectives. Taking our Ocean Water Company, a matrix of corporate goals and objectives could be set up as shown in Figure 4–4.

Training

Quality education for all levels of management and employees is a crucial part of the TQM process. This is one area where the guru is invaluable—helping to lay out the "tools" training (Figure 4–5).

Figure 4-4   OCEAN WATER COMPANY— STRATEGIC AND TACTICAL OBJECTIVES

STRATEGIC	TACTICAL
Improve Quality and Cost Reduction Performance	Implement TQM Philosophy in 1990
	Improve Quality in All Measurements
	Involve All Employees in Cost Reduction and Quality Improvement
	Improve Personnel Relations and Career Development
	Establish Processes to Avoid Hazardous Materials
	Perform to Meet Contract Requirements
Increase Sales and Earnings	Develop Three New Products
	Establish Environment Cleanup Task Team
	Develop New Regional Sales Force
	Develop New International Sales Force
	Establish Small Customer Sales Focus
Diversify Within Water Business	Establish/Acquire Swimming Pool Business
	Establish Sewage Reprocessing Business
Develop Critical New Technologies	Invest in Essential Engineering Facilities
	Develop Biodegradable Chemicals
	Pursue EPA High-Tech Sewage Project
Increase International Business	Capture More than 20% Share
	Merge with International A&E Firm

Figure 4–5   TQM TOOLS TRAINING

Benchmarking
Brainstorming
Pareto analysis
Cause and effect analysis
Flowcharting
Scatter diagrams
Histograms
SPC charting
Mind mapping
Affinity diagrams
Interrelationship diagrams
Tree diagrams
Prioritization matrices
Matrix diagrams
Process decision program charts
Activity network diagrams
Process analysis techniques
Function analysis techniques
Value analysis techniques
Value engineering
PERT critical path mode (CPM) technique
Quality function deployment
Design of experiments
Taguichi methods
Multivariate analysis
Reliability techniques
Failure mode effects analysis (FMEA)

People Involvement and Rewards

It is imperative that the training process is progressively implemented. It starts with total top management, then supervision, while at the same time training the critical process teams and the corrective action teams. This total training will start to open the eyes of all employees to the fact that management is serious, and that they are looking for total employee involvement for economic survival.

A basic method in the TQM philosophy is *departmental task analysis.* This type of analysis concentrates on (a) who supplies things to us, (b) what we do to add value, and (c) who we serve and who our customer is. This technique breaks down the barriers and illuminates the areas for improvement.

The rewards part is, and can be, handled a myriad of ways. One of the most effective is an *employee suggestion and cost reduction program,* but you should keep the paperwork as simple as possible and process the ideas fast! Also, people need to be present at work to be fully productive; some companies pay special quality or biannual awards for zero absenteeism. And due to the nature of humans, most everyone enjoys wearing special jackets, caps, patches, bags, etc. People still value financial rewards—profit sharing, quality bonuses, and other varied pay methods. But, the main objective is to get *all* employees buying into ownership of the company and the quality of the products and services *they* deliver.

Supplier/Customer Focus

Every person is both a supplier and a customer. And Jim Botlen, CEO of Knight-Ridder newspaper fame, calls his firm's quality focus, "customer obsession" in *Business Month* magazine.[16] He had his doubts about the terminology to use, but settled on customer obsession, because obsession conveys intensity and urgency.

Suppliers should always deliver equal to, or better than, the agreed to quality/specification levels. The relationships with suppliers need to be improved and nurtured over a long time. Several factors need to be considered, including:

1. Reduce the number of suppliers in the procurement base.

2. Concentrate on fewer suppliers with longer term contracts and higher quality standards.

3. Develop a better designed data base system with the selected few.

4. Implement TQM processes and techniques to assist suppliers in reaching almost zero parts/million quality deliveries.

5. Develop a supplier rating system that covers quality, cost, schedule, and management responsiveness.

Customers, like suppliers, should be treated with a "caring" attitude. It's not *what* you do, but *how* you do it. As discussed previously, the departmental task analysis can determine who your customers are and what their requirements are. And always remember, what your customer wants is *value*. And value is quality and reliability at a reasonable price. Customers:

1. Are the most important people in any business.

2. Are not just statistics, but warm-blooded humans like ourselves.

3. Have sensitive feelings.

4. Deserve attentive and courteous treatment.

5. Are the only reason we are in business!

Systems Assurance and Measurements

Experience has shown this author that 100% quality inspection—except under very unusual circumstances—will miss 10% of the defects. Also, if there is a separate inspection group, then sometimes it's a how-many-can-we-get-through them challenge. As part of the TQM process, the quality function of the future should become a systems assurance activity.

The systems assurance activity could include:

- Inspecting for the critically few parts or activities.

- Conducting system audits; e.g., the hiring process, safety, inventory system.

- Conducting management audits (see the description in *Management Audits for Excellence*), published by ASQC Quality Press, 1988.

- Assessing the effectiveness of the TQM measurements described in the next chapter.

- Assessing the cost of unquality as described in Chapter 6.

SUMMARY

Why TQM? Our captains of industry are grossly out of touch with their work force! A study released in September 1989 by Rath and Strong, Inc. revealed what some company surveys have been telling top management. The study was done over a five-year period and consists of a sample of 22,600 employees from many companies. Charles Davis in *Business Week*, October 2, 1989 summarized the results as:

- Some 67% of the hourly workers contended that work is not assessed or redesigned regularly enough to keep employees as productive as possible.

- 57% of all workers polled yearned for an improved climate in their workplaces.

- 46% of the survey participants rated their supervisors as ineffective.[17]

Patience, preparation, and practice are needed. Measurement is an integral part of TQM, and it will require these three elements—at the least—to develop a measurement and cost of unquality methodology. Use the TQM thought process to develop your unique business strategy for economic survival.

Quantify the Process—Measure the Progress 5

You cannot manage what you cannot measure.
You cannot measure what you cannot operationally
define. You cannot operationally define what you do not
understand. You will not succeed if you do not manage.

Defense Systems Management College

WHY MEASURE?

Any job that cannot be measured probably adds no value, is not worth doing, and should be eliminated! The ability to increase yields—in any work cell or situation—with a corresponding decrease in process time, energy, or person power is the key to industrial survival today. But any such performance plan should also center on providing a quality product. It is very important, therefore, to constantly consider both effectiveness and efficiency.

- Effectiveness—The degree to which things are produced that are of the correct quality (zero discrepant) and within the allowed process or flow times.

- Efficiency—The degree to which the system uses the right resources; e.g., no unplanned overtime, additional personnel, or additional equipment.

Both effectiveness and efficiency are considered when establishing measurements. Also, results should be measured, not activities. This is particularly true in an attempt to develop measures of performance for white-collar groups. We do not need more activity, but only the minimum activity needed to produce a desired result. Results count; results are valuable. Results, and results alone, should be measured.

WHITE-COLLAR MEASURES

In the soft world (defined as the administrative areas or white-collar organizations), most managers have given up on developing effective or efficiency measures. In contrast to manufacturing areas, these professional organizations primarily use financial or head count measures.[18]

There are many obstacles to overcome in implementing measures in the white-collar area, and they are classical. People are left out of the measurement setting process, each person is not treated as an individual, and they don't think performance measures are fair. First, involve personnel in the design and development of the measures using the menu of parameters and measures discussed later in this chapter and in Appendix A. Second, use the nominal group theory concept for the team as a whole to establish the measures. Third, use group or team-based measures; and fourth, use a family of indicators. White-collar work is frequently complex with important dimensions of quality, timeliness, cost, and quantity. It is the balance between these attributes that is important. Each measure in the family reveals part of the picture, but not the whole. It is the scores on the balanced range of measures taken together that reveal failure, mediocrity, or excellence.

HUMAN RESOURCES EXAMPLE

In the 1980s, the *industrial relations* organization in most companies became known as *human resources,* with the attendant title of vice president for the person in charge. These organizations are still groping with the idea that you can pour money into automation, robotics, and grandiose computer systems, but without a committed team of well-trained, motivated employees, the machines often do not turn out profits.[19] What might the vision, guidelines, and measurement areas look like for today and for the future within such organizations?

Boosting Revenues

An example of human resources:

vision is	all relates back to
mission is	previous chapters and sections
objectives are	

The vision of the human-resource function is to maximize the utilization and appreciation of people as the most important ingredient in keeping the enterprise competitive.

The mission of human resources is to help unify organizational vision/values into constructive action with two major thrusts: (a) boosting the organization's ability to increase revenues and (b) minimize the organizational costs of doing business while improving the quality of the product and services.

The objectives for boosting revenues and minimizing costs are to:

1. Acquire, orient, train, and counsel top-caliber employees, who contribute to our collective daily and future performance.

2. Focus everyone on our central mission, beliefs, and values— especially mindful of the company's concrete vision for success.

3. Be proactive on major human-resource trends that can affect the business in terms of organizational, or individual, achievement.

4. Develop an up-to-date and informed work force; and help to empower individual initiative.

5. Facilitate the involvment of all employees who want to share their ideas on how the company can perform even better.

Minimizing Costs

1. Promote a work environment that builds the loyalty of employees, reducing staffing and turnover costs.

2. Work to reduce "the cost of conflict" by encouraging teamwork and by maintaining communication channels that positively address major business issues.

3. Maintain cost-effective human resource systems that support everyone in the company, from recruitment to retirement.

4. Identify ways that the corporation can synergize its strengths and reduce costly duplication.

5. Assist in creating organizational structures/systems that expedite, rather than impede, quality work efforts.

IMPROVEMENT MEASURES SURVEY

The TQM ideology started in General Dynamics, Fort Worth Division, in 1981 with a quality improvement program.[20] This process and some of the parameters used were progressively shared with industry in general, through presentations, articles, and briefings to industry associations, such as AIA, NSIA, EIA, ASQC, etc. In late 1985, a QIP measure survey of 67 parameters was sent to companies in the aerospace industry. The survey included parameters, measures, their use, whether the measures were meaningful, and whether they were of major or minor significance. The results of the survey are shown in Table 5–1.[21]

The significant aspects that came out of the survey were:

1. The importance of having and using performance measurements in the aerospace industry was fully recognized.

2. Classic measures of quality control were tracked:
   - Scrap, rework, repair, and nonconformance costs.
   - Purchased parts acceptance rates.
   - Inspection escapes.
   - Indirect head counts and dollars.
   - Absenteeism.
   - Supervisory ratios.

3. Lacking were measures of white-collar tasks and total quality:
   - Engineering measures.
   - Correction of deficiencies and warranties.
   - Technical publications.
   - Invoice/payment documentation errors.
   - Software changes.
   - Pareto analysis of most measures.

MEASUREMENT PARAMETERS

Managers, management teams, and employees need measurement tools. They need data to plan, make decisions, and solve problems. How the data is stored, retrieved, and portrayed will determine the extent to which measurement systems are used to support the management process and guide it towards excellence. Good measurement and performance evaluation systems don't just happen—and their implementation will constantly be resisted by others. They evolve as a result of planned, systematic, and conscious efforts to improve the quality of the end product.

Properly designed measurement and evaluation systems ensure a way to constantly improve performance. Effective measures begin and end in continuous improvement, not just control. To get started, select from the list of parameters in Appendix A, design a system of measurements for your organization, and start on your continuous road to improvement.

Table 5–4   QIP MEASURES SURVEY

Item:	Measure:	Use	Meaningful	Major	Minor
Customer Deficiency RPTs	Number RPTs/Plant Population	11	10	8	2
Overtime	Overtime/Straight Time	14	13	8	7
Nonconformance $$ Impact on Profit	Nonconformance $$/Profit $$	8	10	9	2
Engineering Response	Avg Hrs to Respond to Rqst for Eng Action	3	6	2	4
Engineering Rejection Rate	Rejections/Engineering Design Hours	4	5	3	2
Engineering Nonconformance $$	Engr Nonconformance $$/Total Nonconformance $$	5	4	3	1
Avoidable Engineering Changes	Avoidable Engr Chgs/Tot Engr Releases	3	6	2	3
COD ECPS	COD ECPS/Total ECPS	2	3	2	1
Operational Readiness	MC & FMC Aircraft/Aircraft in Fleet	2	2	0	2
Deviations & Waivers	Deviations & Waivers/Delivered End Items	7	8	4	5
Equipment Cost Savings	Savings vs Equip Cost & 2.5 Year Payback	7	10	3	7
Equipment Cost	Equipment Cost/Cost of Sales	4	4	3	1
Equipment Acquisition	Service Rqsts Behind Sched/Rqsts Ahead of Sched	5	3	1	3
First Time Yield (FAB)	Parts Accept 1st Time/Tot Parts Presented	15	14	12	3
Rework/Repair	Rwk & Rpr Hrs/ Dir Mfg Lab Hrs	19	18	18	0
Scrap	(Scrap Hrs/Dir Lab Hrs) & (Scrap Matl $$/Tot Matl $$)	18	18	16	2
Purchased Items	# Parts Accepted/# Parts Received	20	20	18	2
On-Time Deliveries	On-Time Issues/Production Demands	10	12	8	4
Mod Kit Accpt Rate	Total Accepted/Total Inspected	7	7	4	3

Table 5–4   Continued

Item:	Measure:	Use	Meaningful	Major	Minor
Support Equip Accpt Rate	Total Accepted/Total Inspected	5	6	3	3
Spares Acceptance Rate	Total Accepted/Total Inspected	9	10	6	4
Mod Kit Sched Performance	Actual Deliveries/Scheduled Deliveries	6	6	2	4
Supt Equip Schedule Performance	Actual Deliveries/Scheduled Deliveries	6	5	2	4
Spares Schedule Performance	Actual Deliveries/Scheduled Deliveries	10	9	6	4
Tech Order Schedule Performance	Actual Deliveries/Scheduled Deliveries	5	5	2	3
Technical Order Error Rate	Tech Order Errors/Tech Order Pages	3	3	2	1
Service Reports	Service Rpts Answered on Time/Service Rpts Due	7	6	4	2
DD250 Errors	Erroneous DD250S/Tot DD250S	4	5	1	5
Inspection Escapes	Out-of-Dept Rejections/Tot Inspections	12	14	9	5
Major Rejections	Major Rejection Documents/Direct Labor Hrs	9	9	7	3
Cadam Errors	Hrs to Correct Cadam Errors/Support Hrs	1	2	1	1
Quality of Deliverable Software	Number of Errors/1000 Bytes of Code	1	4	3	1
Abnormal Termination of Batch Sys	Batch Abends/Production CPU Time	1	1	0	2
Abnormal Termination of Online Sys	Online Abends/Online Transactions	1	1	0	2
Proposes Responsiveness	Delinquent Proposals/Proposals in Work	9	7	3	5
Journal Voucher Errors	Vouchers in Error/Tot Vouchers	3	3	2	1
Invoice Collections	Invoice $$ Older Than 30 Days/Accts Rec $$	10	9	3	6

Table 5–4   Continued

Item:	Measure:	Use	Meaningful	Major	Minor
Indirect Dollars	Tot Indirect $$/Tot Direct Dollars	14	12	6	8
Absenteeism	Tot Hrs Absent/Tot Hrs Sched.	16	15	9	7
Indirect Headcount	Tot Indirect Headcount/Tot Direct Headcount	19	16	9	8
Travel Costs	Travel $$/Cost of Sales $$	4	4	2	3
Supervisory Ratio	Tot Employees/Tot Supervisors	15	13	7	7
Suggestion Program	Employee Suggestions/Total Employees	9	9	2	7
Cost Reduction Program	Cost Reduction $$/Cost of Sales	9	10	8	2
Nonconformance Costs	Tot Nonconformance $$/Tot Manufacturing $$	17	18	15	3
Rework/Repair Labor	Rework & Repair Labor $$/Tot Manufacturing Labor $$	18	17	16	1
Scrap Material	Scrap Material $$/Tot Material $$	13	14	12	2
Scrap Labor	Scrap Labor $$/Tot Manufacturing Labor $$	12	13	11	2
Scrap/Rwk/Rpr Processing Costs	Srr Processing Support $$/Tot Manfacturing Labor $$	8	9	6	4
Overtime	Tot Overtime Hrs/Tot Hours Worked	16	13	9	7
Major Rejection Documents	Rej Docs Requiring Corrective Action/Tot Rej Docs	6	4	3	2
Major Rejection Costs	Rej $$ Requiring Corrective Action/Tot Rej $$	3	2	2	0
Rejections Per Hour	Number Rejection Documents/1000 Manhours	6	6	5	1
Age of Open Rejections	Rej Open Over 120 Days Per Month/Rej Initiated Ea Month	10	10	6	6

Table 5-4 Continued

Item:	Measure:	Use	Meaningful	Major	Minor
Rejections Per Parts Mfg	Tot Parts Rejected During Mfg/Parts Mfg	9	8	8	1
DD250 Performance	Avg Hrs Between Last Inspection/FLT to DD250	0	0	0	0
Zero Defect Program	Zero Discrepant Products Delivered/Tot Manufactured	3	2	2	1
Flight Inspection	No. Flights to Acceptance/Number of Aircraft	2	2	1	0
Flight Discrepancies Per Flight	Avg. No. Flight Discrepancies/Number of Flights	1	1	1	1
Flight Aborts	Tot Flight Aborts/Number Flight Attempts	2	2	0	2
Flight Inspection Program	Customer Flight Disc Per Ac/Contractor Flight Disc Per	2	2	0	2
Nonconformance Responsibility	PCT Rej by Responsibility—Supp, GFE, Planning, Eng, Mfg	11	12	11	1
Low Dollar Scrap	Tot Low Dollar Scrap $$/Tot Mfg $$	6	6	2	5
Standard Repairs	Number Std Repairs/1000 Mfg Hrs	6	4	3	2
Could Not Duplicate	Number of Units Tested Cnd/Tot Tested Units Rejected	3	3	0	3
Other Losses	Other Material Loss $$/Tot Manufacturing $$	2	3	2	1
Engineering Obsolescence	Engr Obsolescence $$/Tot Manufacturing $$	3	3	0	4

Number of Respondents—21

CHASING A MOVING TARGET

Achieving the Malcolm Baldrige National Quality Award is the ultimate measurement for any enterprise. In 1988, there were three top achievers out of more than 60 applicants—Motorola, Westinghouse, and Globe Metallurgical. In 1989, the number of applicants was just over 40. Out of that number, only two achieved superior products or services—Xerox and Milliken.

David Kearns, chief executive officer, Xerox Corporation, and chairman, National Quality Month, 1989, expressed how Xerox achieved the Baldrige Award.[22] Xerox's obsession with quality started in the 1983–1984 timeframe when Xerox's share of U.S. copier shipments dropped to a low 10% market share! Their solution was a massive, long-term effort to embed quality into every crevice of the organization and to make continuous quality improvement a way of life.

"Going from theory to practice consisted of five important and interrelated ingredients.

1. Total commitment of senior management. First and foremost, senior management must have a long-term commitment to quality. Managers must prove their ability to establish and attain strategic quality goals. They must be able to foster teamwork in and among units and reward individuals for their quality contributions. As a matter of fact, Xerox has a policy that senior managers are promoted on their ability to act as role models for the entire corporation. The bottom line is that when senior management is committed to quality improvement, the company can more easily attain other measures of a successful business.

2. Quantifiable standards and measurements. I cannot emphasize the second factor in our quality improvement strategy enough. Use quantifiable standards and measurements for the way you do business. Companies that don't use measurement tools to identify and solve problems operate in a culture that can only "ready, fire, aim." Take advantage of statistics so that you can ready, aim, and then fire. This is something our competitors in the Far East do particularly well. They use statistics to analyze root causes of problems so that they can be fixed once and for all. We need to emulate the Japanese more in this regard.

   Also be sure to take a good, hard look at yourself and at your competitors on an ongoing basis. Every organization— from administration to product development—should use competitive benchmarking to meet its targets in terms of customer satisfaction, cost, reliability, product development time, and return on assets. Benchmarking is the continuous process in which you measure your services, processes, and products against direct competitors and recognized leaders.

Determine the cost and reliability aspects of these companies' products. Decide if—and why—their products and services are better than yours. Measure your rate of improvement against theirs. In other words, benchmark everything against the industry leaders to help you learn what makes the best companies superior.

3. Education and training. You need more than a strong commitment and statistics to help keep your competitive edge. Your quality improvement strategy should address the needs of your greatest resource of all: your employees.

   To help employees reach their full potential, Xerox began implementing a company-wide training program in 1984. Courses covered the corporate mission and goals, problem-solving techniques, and the quality improvement process.

   Training sessions started with senior management and spread down the company—a first for Xerox. Every manager went through comprehensive training twice; once as a student and once as a teacher. Managers were trained with their peers and were then held responsible for training their employees.

   At this point, virtually all of the 100,000 employees (from boardroom to factory floor) have been trained. They are now able to do their jobs better than ever.

4. Recognition and rewards. Another key ingredient in a quality improvement strategy is to establish programs that help ensure that employees continue to work in an innovative and creative environment in which their ideas and contributions are recognized and rewarded.

   In times such as these when so many companies are downsizing, it is more important than ever that people derive job satisfaction from their current positions. To this end, one of Xerox's philosophies is to empower people.

   Let employees know that you value their ideas. Discuss the reasons why the company can (or cannot) implement their suggestions. Give employees the autonomy to develop ideas and suggestions—and reward those who do. Allow people to experience failures as well as successes. Let them know that it is okay to take risks, and that it is okay to take risks and fail—if the risks were legitimate.

Directly involve employees in solving problems and issues. In line with our commitment to empower people, 75% of our work force is involved in more than 8,000 problem-solving teams around the world. Assess employees on their willingness and ability to improve quality. In addition to reviews where you recognize employee strengths, you may wish to give cash awards and other types of bonuses to employees who significantly contribute to meeting quality improvement targets. Just as important, though, catch employees doing something right. Thank people for doing their jobs well.

5. Effective and consistent communication. Effective communication is the fifth key factor in our *leadership through quality* strategy. Employees must understand the corporate goals and how the company intends to meet customer expectations. They must also know what their job objectives are and how those objectives fit into the broader corporate objectives. Knowing this type of information helps motivate employees by making their jobs more meaningful.

Utilize every medium available (discussion groups, multimedia presentations, printed materials) to help provide continuous and consistent messages within and among divisions.

One exceptional way to foster effective communication is to hold teamwork days where teams have the opportunity to display and discuss their best work. Teamwork days provide an excellent opportunity for employees, customers, and suppliers to exchange valuable ideas and information.

Here are a few hard facts from six years of effort:

- Reduced average manufacturing costs by over 20% despite inflation.
- Reduced the time it takes to bring a new product to market by as much as 60%.
- Substantially improved the quality of our products. *Dataquest* rates Xerox products as No. 1 in five out of six market segments.
- Increased revenue for employees by 20%.
- Decreased nonconforming parts from 8% to less than 0.03%.
- Decreased billing errors from 3.5% to 0.3%.
- And, perhaps, the first American company in an industry targeted by the Japanese to regain market share. And we did it without the aid of tariffs or protection of any kind.

The focus on quality that Xerox initiated five years ago was built on some very fundamental assumptions about the American worker:

- That management does not have all the answers.
- That all people have ideas about how their work can be done more effectively.
- That people closest to the problems often have the best solutions.
- That this almost unlimited source of knowledge and creativity can be tapped through employee involvement.
- That people are willing and eager to share their thoughts and participate in developing solutions to business problems."

SUMMARY

Perhaps the best way to summarize this chapter is to quote and use liberally from the recent Conference Board Research Bulletin No. 224.[23]

"Until a few years ago, when U.S. business began to perceive foreign competition as a more serious threat, quality was taken pretty much for granted. Most companies did not have broad quality programs. More typical, quality considerations arose in the context of manufacturing as, e.g., the need to inspect and test parts and assemblies on a production line. But the growing influx of competitive imports perceived by consumers to be of superior quality to those domestically produced forced a radical reappraisal of quality. This, in turn, led to the recognition that quality concerns are as important in service industries as in manufacturing, and that quality awareness should apply throughout a company's organization, not only in areas that directly affect customers."

Today, a growing number of companies make a concerted effort to eliminate error from the design, production, marketing, distribution, and servicing of all kinds of products and services. Many executives now believe that quality performance and continual quality improvement are the keys to the productivity, profitability—and even the survival—of much of U.S. business."

The concept of measuring quality is relatively new to U.S. firms. Companies that responded to the survey by the Conference Board employ the following techniques to assess quality.[23] To measure customer perceptions:

- Satisfaction surveys (the most common approach).
- Feedback from customers, including interviews, executives' visits, and salespersons' field reports.
- Information developed in customers' focus groups.
- Complaint statistics.
- Billing adjustments granted to customers.
- Standards of service (airline).
- Warranty analysis.
- Benchmark studies (i.e., comparison of one's own performance or results with that of a competitor whose performance is known to be excellent).
- Comparison of shipping dates versus customers' requests.
- Reports of product tests.

To measure profitability:

- Reports of quality costs including, for example, the cost of complaints, scrap, waste, and rework.
- Financial reports to management (sometimes presented on control charts); e.g., net income before and after taxes, profit margins, operational cash flow.
- Ratio analysis of financial reports (e.g., return on equity, return on invested capital, return on sales, net income before taxes as a percent of sales).
- Cost/benefit analysis.

To measure productivity:

- Statistics on yields, throughput, volume, efficiency, etc.
- Inventory turnover.
- Value of production.
- Statistics on labor output.
- Overhead trends (improved quality may result in lower overhead).
- Ratio of product costs to revenue.

- Cost reports of various kinds.
- Downtime.
- Schedule compliance.
- On-time delivery.
- Time and money saved on projects.
- Production cycle time.

To measure employee morale:

- Summaries and reports of attitude surveys (by far the most common).
- Analysis of information derived from focus groups and other employee feedback.
- Results of one-on-one interviews.
- Statistics on turnover, absenteeism, complaints, and suggestions (favorable trends indicate probable improvements in quality).

To measure market share (based on the assumption that improvements in quality will result in a greater share of the market):

- Business and industry statistics.
- Surveys.
- Market analysis.
- Contracts won and lost.
- Consultants' studies.

Quantifying quality costs is a very new concept for most companies. The Big 6 accounting firms are starting to consult on this subject, and it is slowly creeping into accounting literature. And that's what Chapter 6 is all about.

Cost of Unquality   6

Let it be said:
'It was done right,
It was done well.'
Perfection must be
Your credo of work
And quality your
way of life.

Konstantin

THE LOSS FUNCTION

World class managers are recognizing the need for better quality systems and are implementing quality improvement programs at a greater rate than ever. However, in the TQM environment, they are not changing management and accounting structures to reflect these new TQM requirements. Mostly, managers are still rated on how much they do—not how efficiently they produce.

Current systems must be changed to a strategic emphasis away from product control toward process control; away from how much toward how efficiently. Failure to implement an overall defect prevention philosophy results in a corporate clash of philosophies. If you have started a TQM process you will already have seen this clash. If you are starting your journey, then make sure you put up the antenna to prevent this clash from derailing the process. It is imperative that the TQM philosophy base decisions on measurable units, not opinions, conjecture, or personalities. To technical personnel, units mean almost anything quantifiable; but to management units mean only one thing—dollars. Carefully compare the material listed next to how the function is handled in your company; perhaps this many and more organizations exist that add no value to the total function that they perform. Many activities have been established, such as rework/repair stations that would be eliminated if the manufacturing processes were "do it right the first time." These activities should be some of the processes to be examined by cross-functional Critical Process Teams (CPT) to eliminate this waste or non-value added organizations.

Organizations Established to Manage Waste

- Engineering liaison
- Planning liaison
- Tool design liaison
- Inspection
- Corrective action board
- Material review board
- Supplier surveillance

- Change control board
- Material coordinators/expeditors
- Time card auditors
- Idle time surveyors
- Finance labor auditors
- Salvage operations
- Rework/repair stations

The Tools of Waste

- Quality assurance report
- Quality completion order
- Inspection cleanup sheet
- Low dollar scrap
- Inspection hold tag
- Loss and obsolescence report
- Quality deficiency report
- Material deficiency report
- Material survey action report
- Request for material survey
- One-time inspection
- Material survey stock location and quantity report
- Material survey purge notice
- Failure analysis report
- Flight squawks

- Shortage meetings
- Material receipt discrepancy notice
- Corrective action request
- Field service report
- Service report
- Parts failure and service difficulties report
- Planning trouble and action book
- Minor deviation authorization
- Incomplete task log
- Inspection test request
- Vendor part rework order
- Request for engineering action
- Engineering change notice
- Time Compliance Technical Orders (TCTO)
- Warranty claims

Classic quality cost systems have been written about extensively, such as the books and articles published by ASQC, Crosby, Juran, and other quality "gurus." The four categories—prevention, appraisal, internal failures, and external failure costs—have been fairly well defined. However, these classic cost of quality categories show only a portion of the true cost of unquality, and the categories are not widely used by upper management. The costs of unquality are those internal and external costs that happen in every organization. These failure costs are defects that happen because people are not adequately trained, work processes are not well known, data collection systems do not track the failures, and the financial systems do not cost them. It has been estimated that 15% to 30% of sales are lost to "poor quality." This author's studies show this to be in the ballpark of about 5% to 15% as shown in Figure 6–1, as discussed below, and as depicted by Figure 6–2.

THE MODEL

> In a utopian world—
> workers always perform correctly
> materials have no flaws
> products always work perfectly.
>
> In the real world—
> people make errors
> equipment malfunctions
> Ivory soap is only 99.44% pure.

The difference described in the quote illustrates the cost of unquality, and the reason for a methodology for measuring this cost. Within the aerospace industry, traditional "quality costs" account for less than 2% of sales dollars. But the *unquality costs* could account for up to 15% of total sales dollars!

Figure 6–1 depicts a company with $500 million in annual sales. The cost of unquality has been reduced from 15% in 1986 to the current level of 6% in 1988. That's still a staggering $30 million that's going essentially to inefficiency and ineffectiveness or waste! The percentages and cost are:

- Design—21.5% and $6.45 million.
- Manufacturing—52% and $15.60 million.
- Supplier—15% and $4.50 million.
- Field or warranty—6.5% and $1.95 million.
- Administrative—5.0% and $1.50 million.

Figure 6-1   Cost of Unquality

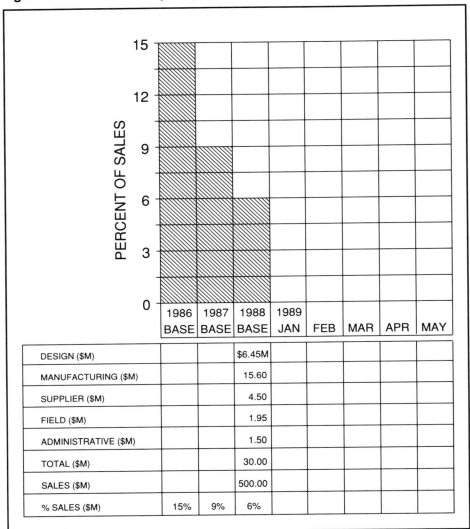

DESIGN ($M)			$6.45M					
MANUFACTURING ($M)			15.60					
SUPPLIER ($M)			4.50					
FIELD ($M)			1.95					
ADMINISTRATIVE ($M)			1.50					
TOTAL ($M)			30.00					
SALES ($M)			500.00					
% SALES ($M)	15%	9%	6%					

Figure 6-2   Cost of Unquality Model

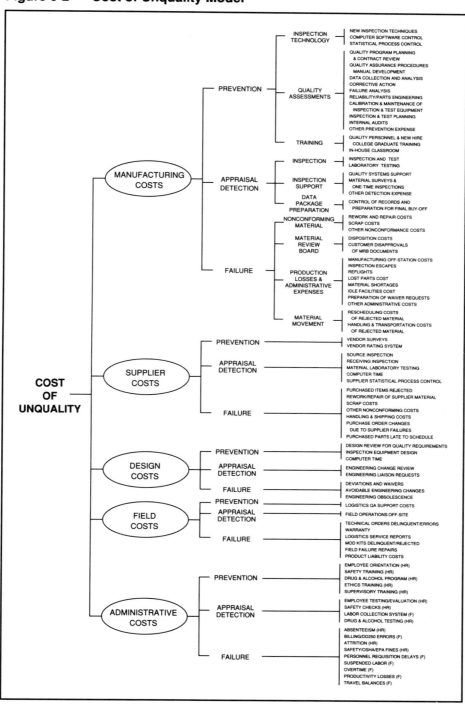

The road to implementing TQM and its subset measurement system is full of potholes crafted by those who resist change or the neo-cultists of turf protectors. The TQM steering committee should immediately set the establishment of a cost of unquality model as one of their critical process team activities. Figure 6–2 shows a sample total cost of unquality model. More areas can be added to the model as the critical process team progresses into the total quality continuous improvement process.

Design Costs

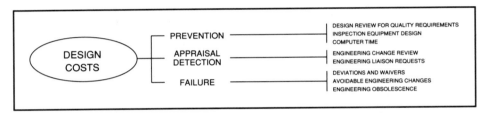

All goodness or evil either starts in marketing or engineering! If the process is not well defined, tracked, and measured in the design function, then the problems will cascade all the way to the customers—or should we say, lack of customers—who buy the product. This is highlighted by the concurrent engineering process used by Japanese versus U.S. firms' approach to engineering changes. The concurrent engineering process coordinates all functions up front to eliminate changes that take place as and after the design is released (Figure 6–3).

The author has looked at the design process and at the reasons for avoidable engineering changes at General Dynamics, Fort Worth; General Dynamics, Convair, and Martin-Marietta, Denver. It was significant that all three companies had an approximate 49% error in the design process. As noted in Figure 6–4, the reason codes A, C, and E are error factors that cause the unquality loss. If you add the figures up, they total 47%; the second company was 50.2%, and the third company was 49.8%.

Using the design costs model we can now estimate the costs of these avoidable engineering change notices (ECNs).

The number of avoidable ECNs _____
× Average hours to work _____
× EN labor rate _____
× EN burden rate _____
Total cost $ _____

Figure 6-3 COMPARISON OF JAPANESE AND U. S. ENGINEERING CHANGE PROCESSES

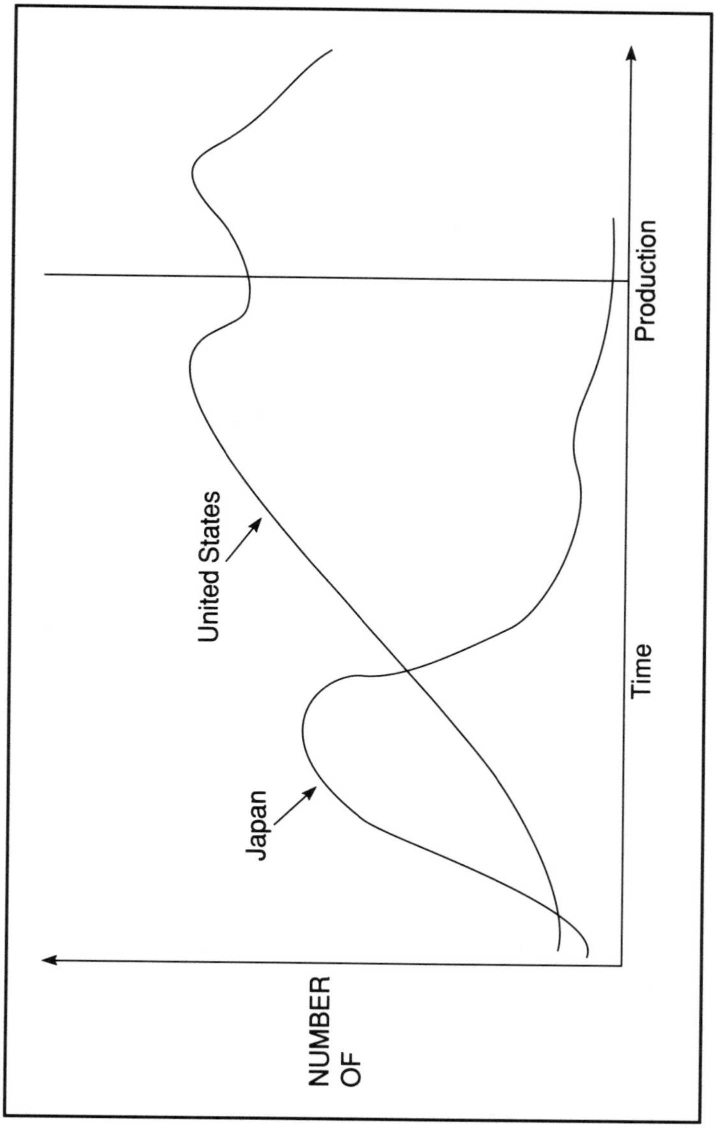

(Source: Department of Defense TQM Manual 5000.5IG.)

Figure 6-4   ECN CODES BY PERCENTAGE

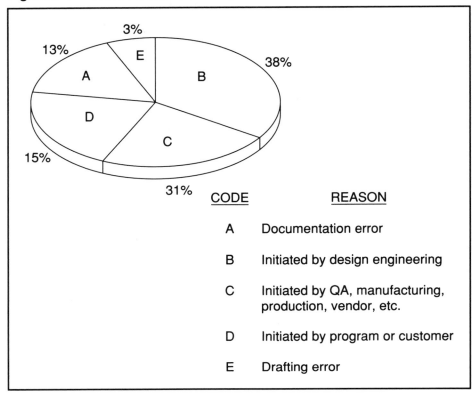

CODE	REASON
A	Documentation error
B	Initiated by design engineering
C	Initiated by QA, manufacturing, production, vendor, etc.
D	Initiated by program or customer
E	Drafting error

Oliver Boileau, past president of General Dynamics, in an interview with Dr. H. James Harrington, stated that the process illustrated here saved General Dynamics, Fort Worth almost $17.5 million in 1984.[24]

Another large item that most companies overlook or for which the costs are buried, is engineering obsolescence. Engineering obsolescence is the dollar value of production parts that are determined unreworkable or unusable due to engineering changes.

Because design engineering is not done "concurrently" with program management, production, quality, materials, and logistics (Figure 6–5), the changes are too many and too late; this causes a great deal of additional effort by engineering change review boards. The engineering change review extra costs are computed as follows:

$$
\begin{aligned}
&\text{Number of ECNs} \underline{\hspace{1.5cm}}\\
\times\ &\text{Average hours per ECN} \underline{\hspace{1.5cm}}\\
\times\ &\text{Engineering labor rate} \underline{\hspace{1.5cm}}\\
\times\ &\text{Engineering burden rate} \underline{\hspace{1.5cm}}\\
&\text{Total cost \$} \underline{\hspace{1.5cm}}
\end{aligned}
$$

Figure 6-5 CONCURRENT ENGINEERING PROGRAM

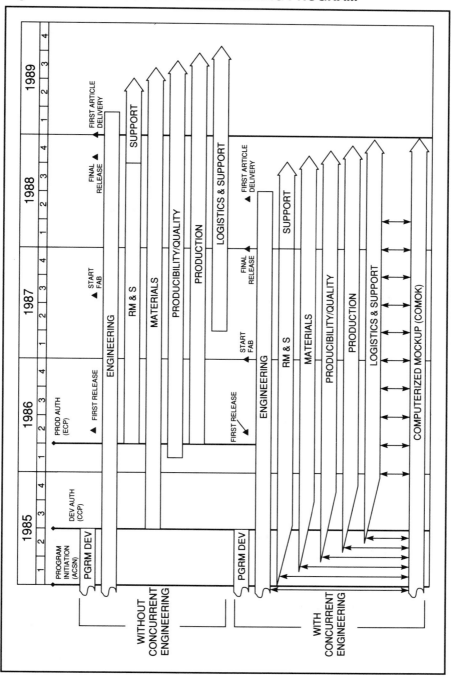

(Source: General Dynamics, Fort Worth, TX)

As a result of the lack of concurrent engineering design, the amount of engineering liaison requests from tooling, the materials' purchasing group, and the production floor are voluminous. Engineering liaison request (ELR) costs are computed as follows:

$$
\begin{aligned}
\text{Number of ELRs} &\ \underline{\hspace{1.5cm}} \\
\times\ \text{Average hours per ELR} &\ \underline{\hspace{1.5cm}} \\
\times\ \text{Engineering labor rate} &\ \underline{\hspace{1.5cm}} \\
\times\ \text{Engineering burden rate} &\ \underline{\hspace{1.5cm}} \\
\text{Total cost \$} &\ \underline{\hspace{1.5cm}}
\end{aligned}
$$

Supplier Costs

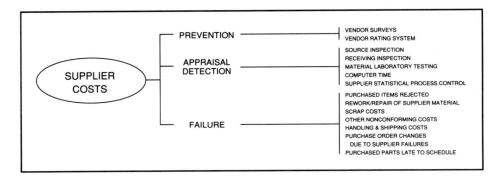

Typically, a manufacturing firm purchases 50% to 60% of the product. This is usually tracked and purchased in two or three categories—standard hardware of fasteners, electrical connectors, electronic piece parts, wire, etc.; large structures of forgings, castings, extrusions, and other metal- and plastic-formed parts; and line replaceable units (LRUs) or finished subassemblies. Each category has its unique procurement specifications and quality requirements.

In 1984, a study was done by the author for the Aerospace Industries Association concerning vendor/supplier audits. The results as shown in Figure 6–6 are:

- 29% of the government audits on the contractors' suppliers were duplicated.

- 61% of the contractors' audits on their suppliers were duplicated.

In turn, a large effort was started in early 1985 by the DoD, General Dynamics (taking the lead), and many industry associations to create a National Contractors Accreditation System (NCAS). Its purpose was to (a) standardize audits, (b) have an unbiased third party perform annual

Figure 6-6   AUDIT IMPACT/POTENTIAL REDUNDANCY

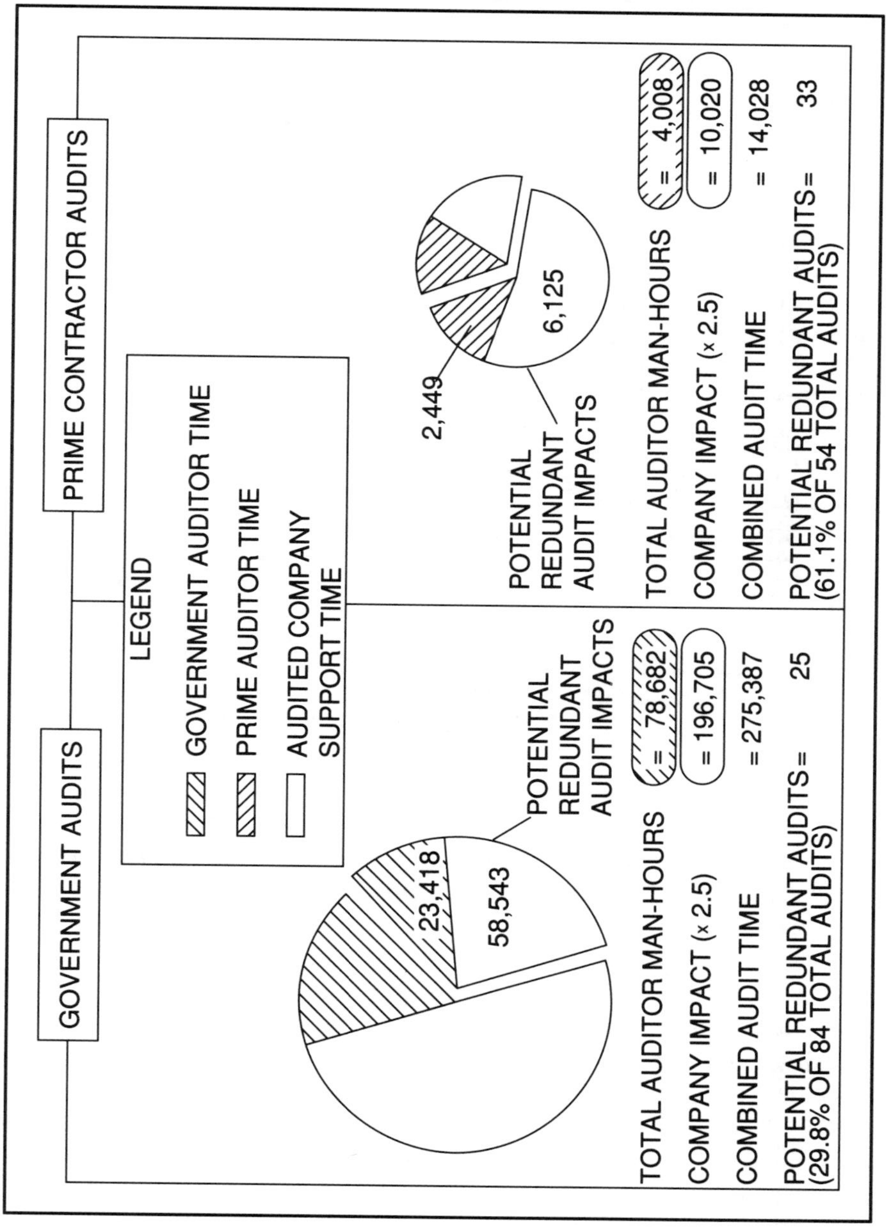

Figure 6-7   PROPOSED CONCEPT FOR NCAS

- SYSTEM ACCREDITATION/PRODUCT CERTIFICATION:
  - •• PROVIDE A LISTING OF SUPPLIERS WITH ACCREDITED QA SYSTEMS FOR USE BY AEROSPACE AND DEFENSE CONTRACTORS AND THE GOVERNMENT.
  - •• QUALIFY PRODUCTS AND PROVIDE A QUALIFIED MANUFACTURER'S LISTING (QML) FOR USE BY AEROSPACE AND DEFENSE CONTRACTORS AND THE GOVERNMENT.
- THE SUPPLIERS/PRODUCTS WOULD BE CERTIFIED BY INDEPENDENT CONSULTANTS/LABORATORIES CONTROLLED AND REGULATED BY A THIRD PARTY AND THE AEROSPACE AND DEFENSE INDUSTRY.
- REQUIREMENTS, CONTROLS, AND APPROVALS PLUS TECHNICAL SUPPORT WOULD BE PROVIDED BY THIRD PARTY, DOD, AND AEROSPACE AND DEFENSE INDUSTRY COMPANIES.
- RECOGNIZED BY THE U.S. GOVERNMENT FOR INDUSTRY USE AND FOR GOVERNMENT USE IN SPARES PROCUREMENT AND DIRECT BUYS.
- MAJOR BENEFIT CONSISTS OF STANDARDIZED CRITERIA AND CONTROLS COUPLED WITH INDUSTRY COST SAVINGS. CONSISTENTLY HIGH QUALITY QML PRODUCTS RESULTING IN INCREASED RELIABILITY IS ANOTHER MAJOR BENEFIT.

audits, (c) improve the quality of products, and (d) cut overall procurement costs to the U.S. government (Figure 6–7). Another study done by the NCAS group revealed that a stunning $210 million was being spent by the aerospace industry auditing the supplier base to meet government specifications and maintain quality of the products. The benefits of NCAS auditing for all parties can be seen in Figure 6–8.

Using the supplier costs model, we can estimate the cost of source inspection. These costs of source inspection include all physical tests, inspections, or procedure surveillance at a supplier's facility by contractor personnel. For one large company, this is more than 50 field personnel in the United States alone, at a cost exceeding $2.2 million.

Another expensive item is the receiving inspection function. These costs are accumulated from the identified payroll, any rejection documents, special laboratory tests, retesting of electrical/electronics piece parts, and any retesting caused by failures of supplier hardware as a result of higher level system tests. From one contractor's data, this cost is approximately $27 million and involves more than 200 personnel!

Figure 6-8   Benefits of a National Contractors Accreditation System

o **SUPPLIER**
- VERY LITTLE CONTRACTOR/ OEM INTERFACE
- NO QML PRODUCT INSPECTION DELAYS
- OPPORTUNITY TO STANDARDIZE REQUIREMENTS
- SINGLE INTERPRETATION OF REQUIREMENTS
- SIGNIFICANTLY FEWER SURVEYS/AUDITS

o **DOD/AEROSPACE USER**
- IMPROVED PROCUREMENT MANAGEMENT
- INCREASED STANDARDIZATION
- CONSISTENT SURVEILLANCE AND CONTROL TECHNIQUES
- INCREASED USE OF NON-GOVERNMENT STANDARDS

3-way benefits

o **CONTRACTORS/OEMs**
- CONDUCT SIGNIFIGANTLY FEWER SURVEYS/AUDITS
- ON-SITE, IN-PROCESS MONITORING
- IMMEDIATE REACTION TO SUPPLIER PROBLEMS
- MORE TIMELY AND EFFECTIVE CORRECTIVE ACTION
- REDUCED COSTS, INTERNAL AND PQA
- IMPROVED CONTROL OF PROCESSES AND SYSTEMS
- APPROVED QMLs AND SOURCE LISTS

Rejected purchased items can have a very large impact on a company. The number of suppliers, buying at the lowest cost (and not buying for the best value), and shoddy quality of parts are the main contributors to (a) receiving rejections as high as 10%, (b) material surveys and one-time inspections in the production line due to inspection escapes or no inspections at all, (3) and as high as 50% fallout when the items see their first system test or acceptance test procedure (ATP) (Figure 6–9). Aerospace companies' data show 50% to 70% ATP failure rates for valves, radios, radars, complex subassemblies, etc. Purchased items rejected costs out as:

Number of supplier rejection documents _____
× Cost per rejection _____
Total cost $ _____

Rework and repair of supplier material are costs to the company to rework or repair and retest to restore the items to blueprint specifications or allowable deviations.

Supplier repair/rework hours by company _____
× Manufacturing burden rate _____
Total cost $ _____

Other manufacturing costs are the costs of labor by non-hands-on personnel; i.e., planners, production specialists, expediters, re-inspection personnel, and data processing personnel. All these people charge to the rejection documentation, which all have unique labor charging codes:

Figure 6–9   EQUIPMENT QUALITY EVALUATION
REMOVAL ACTIVITY

RR: REMOVAL RATE%

RMMH: RELATIVE MAINTENANCE MAN-HOURS PER REMOVAL

APR		NOV-APR		APR		
RR %	QTY	RR %	QTY	RMMH	NOMENCLATURE	SUPPLIER
47	10	40	9.8	15.2	Computer	
33	7	26	5.5	23.3	Electronic Unit	
30	6	27	5.7	5.2	Data Unit	
30	6	19	3.5	2.0	Formed Sheet Metal	
26	5	25	5.3	5.9	Electronic Display	
22	4	35	8.2	3.5	Tape Cartridge	
22	4	06	1.0	6.4	Antenna	
21	3	25	5.2	4.2	Electronic Generator	
18	3	17	3.2	7.4	Computer	
18	3	18	3.3	6.8	Computer	

Total other supplier nonconformance costs _____
× Manufacturing burden rate _____
Total cost $ _____

Naturally, the obvious answer is to find and track as many cost elements as possible to change the system of doing business: Select fewer suppliers, work with them on a long-term basis, influence them to install a TQM process using all the tools of statistical process control and improve their quality output.

Manufacturing Costs

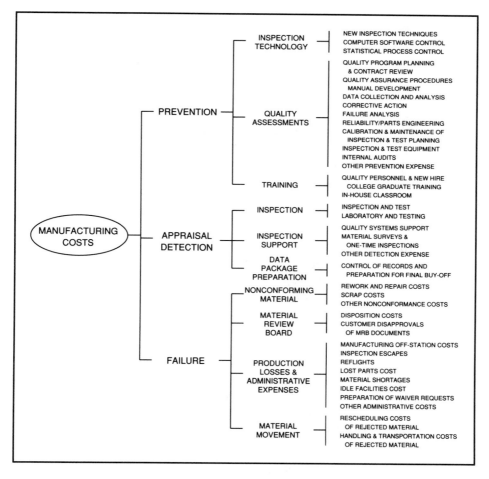

The manufacturing function is usually tracked more closely with more attributes, thus its percentage of loss is larger—in the model, it is 52% or $15.6 million (Figure 6–1). Several elements of the manufacturing function will be discussed, one or two from each element of prevention costs, appraisal costs, and failure costs.

- Prevention costs—These costs can best be described by one of the TQM tools: *statistical process control* (SPC). The cost is calculated by taking all costs of running and reporting the quality data system (which includes systems engineering, developing techniques, processing, and computer operations) and multiplying by 75%; 75% is the proportional amount that is caused by failures in manufacturing. Add to this the salaries and training costs of implementing SPC. This cost can be fairly large, especially starting into SPC.

- Another prevention cost element is failure analysis. This cost is collected from two different streams of data:
  (1) All costs associated with the examination of defective items to determine extent and causes—costs for corrective action, including salaries and wages of personnel for cause of defects, failure analysis, and corrective action.
  (2) Costs for reliability/parts engineering, including specialized disciplines to improve product integrity and performance.
  These two cost elements all add to $4.4 million.

- Appraisal/Detection Costs—There are many things that escape the procurement receiving inspection or manufactured inspection. A system has to be in place to handle these escapes; it's usually called a material survey/one-time inspection system (MS/OTI). Such a system has been used most effectively by General Dynamics in the F-16 worldwide coproduction program in 11 countries and 69 coproduction companies. The MS-OTI system consists of a process of locating suspected defective parts identified by the quality defect control system. A unique work order or cost account charge number is established for use by every function involved in locating the defective parts. They have to be located, identified, and pulled from the parts location, work in process, or the product. The suspected parts have to be replaced, reworked, or returned to the supplier. This cost element is derived as follows:

Number of material surveys _____
× Hours required to complete survey _____
× Production labor rate _____
× Production burden rate _____
Subtotal A $ _____

Number of one-time inspections _____
× Hours required for inspection _____
× Engineering labor rate _____
× Engineering burden rate _____
Subtotal B $ _____

Subtotal A + Subtotal B = Total cost.

If the quality system and this methodology does not prevent the hardware from being shipped to the customers, then the result can be disaster. A time compliance technical order (in military language) or a product recall must then be instituted—a product recall usually has about 10 times the dollar impact of an internal MS/OTI, plus perhaps partial erosion of market share of the product.

- Failure Costs—In the manufacturing arena, the hidden factor of scrap, rework, and repair costs can be 2% to 5% of sales (Figure 6–10). These are the costs of scrap, including the costs of labor and material, and rework and repair, including the costs of manufacturing and retesting to restore the articles to specifications or allowable deviations.

Field Costs

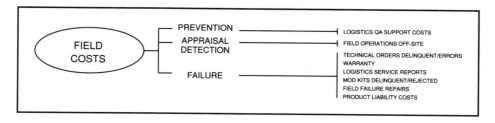

The process of developing and producing the operating, maintenance, and repair manuals for any product is a significant challenge for an organization. And if they are not correct, then product liability costs can be staggering, especially in the public transportation and medical fields. The cost of technical orders delinquent/errors can be calculated as follows:

Number of errors _____
× Cost of producing a page _____
× Engineering labor rate _____
× Engineering burden rate _____
Subtotal A $ _____

Figure 6-10 QUALITY PERFORMANCE TRENDS: Nonconformance Hours

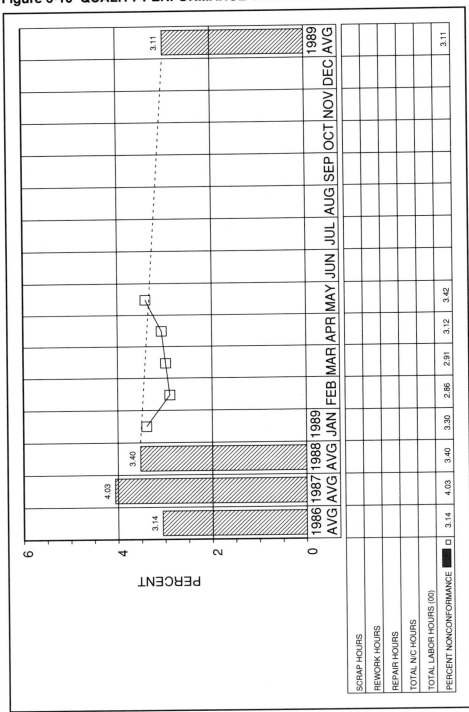

Number TOs delinquent _____
× Time to expedite _____
× Engineering labor rate _____
× Engineering burden rate _____
Subtotal B $ _____

Subtotal A + Subtotal B = Total cost.

Warranty or recall costs can be staggering if defective products get in the hands of the customer/user. The redesign and replacement kits' manufacturing time can also mean the costs of non-use of the airplane, the system, etc:

Warranty costs = Total cost.

Modification kits delinquent/rejected can add additional costs to the warranty costs:

Number of kits delinquent _____
× Time required to expedite _____
× Manufacturing labor rate _____
× Manufacturing burden rate _____
Subtotal A $ _____

Number of kits rejected _____
× Time required to correct _____
× Manufacturing labor rate _____
× Manufacturing burden rate _____
Subtotal B $ _____

Subtotal A + Subtotal B = Total cost.

Administrative Costs

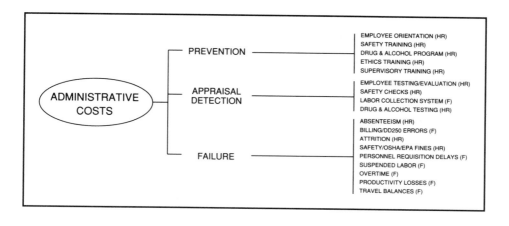

When you employ TQM and have pursued all of the non-value added costs, then one particular administrative cost becomes very important. Effectiveness and efficiency can only be obtained when you have a well-trained and necessary work force. The number of days to process employee requisitions to hire a required person are the costs calculated as:

Average number of days to process the requisition _____
× 8 hours per day _____
× Overtime average cost per hour _____
× Number of requisitions delayed over 10 days _____
× The burden rate _____
Total cost $ _____

Labor reporting errors, especially in the government contracting arena, cause loss of revenue to the company. Errors are made either on manual reporting cards or incorrectly entered into the automated, electronic system. This causes the labor to be put into a suspense file, and then the detective work starts to find the correct codes and also, why it happened. These anomalies in the process are estimated to be 2% to 5%. This is the same "scrap/rework/repair" syndrome that goes on in the production departments.

Number of reporting and time card errors (hours lost) _____
× Approximate cost per burden pool _____
Subtotal A $ _____

Suspended labor hours (14 days) _____
× Prime rate for borrowing costs _____
Subtotal B $ _____

Subtotal A + Subtotal B = Total cost.

Absenteeism is a pox on U.S. industry. Some studies have shown that the United States has a higher absenteeism rate than most other industralized nations. It characteristically is running at an average of 5%. Absenteeism occurs when workers—salaried or hourly—are not at the workplace for their intended purpose. Vacation, military leave, and bereavement leave are not considered as absence. But 5% of 2,008 hours is about 100 hours per year.

Hours absent _____
× Hourly (or daily) rate (burdened) _____
× General and administrative rate _____
Total cost $ _____

SUMMARY

The bottom line for any business is profit. It is the blood that keeps the system going. Without profits, the business cannot stay alive as an ongoing concern, cannot invest in its future, and cannot expand into existing or new markets.

If you could find a way to get 5% to 15% of your sales into the profit pool, what could happen? First, it would make you much more competitive and because of these efficiency improvements, the pricing of your products could be greatly enhanced. Ask Motorola how they are doing with their Six-Sigma Quality and the impact it has had on their pagers and cellular telephone products. Second, the possible 100% to 300% increase in profits could be partially passed on to the owners/shareholders. Third, research and development could be increased making the company's future better. Fourth, employees should share in the enhanced return of their efforts, and thus, their attitudes toward the company would improve. And fifth, it would help this nation in its strategic position in the world's marketplace.

Leadership—The Survival Link! 7

A man looked at the heavenly gate,
his face was scarred and wrinkled.
He stood before the man of fate
and asked admission to the fold.
"What have you done," Saint Peter asked,
"to gain admission here?"
"I've been battling government bureaucracies,"
he said, "for many and many a year."
The pearly gate swung open wide,
and Saint Peter touched the bell.
"Come in and choose your harp," he said.
"You've had your share of hell!"

D. J. Talley,
Colonel, USAF (Ret.)
1980

THE ROARING MOUSE

There are two major factors that set big companies apart from small companies. First is their high number of drones or conservators. These are the people who don't want to rock the boat. They have a comfortable, predictable existence, and they want to keep it that way. Companies vary in their concentration of drones. The ones with the smaller numbers prosper, while larger numbers of conservators can kill a company. Smaller companies simply cannot afford to have drones.[25]

The second major factor hits big business because it is big. Lockheed has nearly 100,000 employees, but no matter how many Skunk Works (special projects free of bureaucracy) it has, it is difficult to use the same techniques all the time with those 100,000 employees. The size of a company can create such a bureaucracy with its multiple layers of management that a problem can occur at a lower level before upper management has a chance for preventive action.

Norman Augustine, chairman of Martin-Marietta, quantified this management problem when he was at the DoD—another big, big company. He found that each level of required approval *doubled* the time needed for a decision. Starting with half a day for one approval level, Augustine found that 13 levels of approval need 4,100 days or about 11 years! Under these circumstances, big government programs are guaranteed to be obsolete before they are fielded, let alone before completely operational.

The larger the organization, the longer the approval cycle and the fewer decisions that can be made. A dynamic leader/achiever can make a difference, but sooner or later, he or she will be swamped by the numbers—thus innovation cools, and the innovative people start deserting the sinking ship.

WE ARE FLUNKING

The Massachusetts Institute of Technology (MIT) recently released a study that is a stinging indictment of U.S. management practices and attitudes.[26] The dirty half-dozen weaknesses it found were:

- Outdated strategies and parochial thinking.
- Short-time horizons.
- Technological attitudes that favor invention over production.
- Neglect of human resources, specifically education—"perhaps our biggest weakness."

- Failures of cooperation, both within companies and between a company and its suppliers.

- Government and industry operate at cross-purposes, oblivious to each other's goals.

To correct these weaknesses in the face of three long-term trends— globalization; the demand for higher-quality, more-sophisticated products; and rapid technological advances—MIT urges industry, government, and education to follow five imperatives:

- Focus on producing "the new way," and stop putting finance ahead of production.

- Cultivate a new "economic citizenship" that gives individuals more responsibility.

- Blend cooperation and individualism by flattening organizations.

- Learn to live in a world economy.

- Provide for the future by investing heavily in basic education and technical literacy.

A search for the systemic, root cause of this cancer uncovers but one: *management* attitudes. Since we have ignored the overwhelming evidence of the 1980s, just what will it take to shed antiquated ideas and methodologies, and forge ahead of the rest of the world?

ACHIEVERS LEAD

Leadership has three or four definitions, depending on which dictionary one uses, but they are all very bland and nondescript; e.g., "the capacity to lead." Now look up *achievement*, "a result, something accomplished as by superior ability, special effort, or great valor." This definition is marked by distinction.

How many executives think about their jobs in terms of valor? What most people do is confuse achievement with advancement. However, if you take care of achievement, advancement will take care of itself!

The executive should be an example, should do his or her job in head-turning acts of competence, and should inspire others. Achievers lead well by their performance, they add value to their corporations. "You can't be good at what you do if you don't care, and you can't care if you are not authentic."[27] Your challenge is to be distinctively you—to act on your individual strengths and project them.

VISIONARY LEADERSHIP

Today, the pressure for change is coming from inside the business organization as well as from the outside. It's the individual, not government, that will be the primary instrument for dealing with the problems that confront us. And these achievers' expressions of values will cause our organizations to change.

We are headed toward an era when people will believe in the message stated in the Epilogue, "Good Enough"—only the best will be good enough, not just that's 'good enough.' After 200 years of managing control, people will have to learn how to manage change a bit better than they have done these past two decades.

While changes in leadership and organization culture are moving fast in some companies, the message might better become one of strategy. Visionary leadership, rather than management skills, will be the key to organizations' economic survival. Our future leaders will have to be dynamic, open, caring, available, and, above all, charismatic.

The effective organization of the future will be characterized as a thousand little steps taken by creative, caring, loving, equal people. None of these terms is fully incorporated into everyday management language yet. But even more, one of the new terms we will have trouble dealing with is equality. Although it's the American way, we ignore it when we structure work groups, task teams, or business organizations.[28]

ENTERPRISE EDUCATION

John Stack of Springhall Remanufacturing Corporation (SRC) has a unique approach to teaching and educating his company's employees on the free enterprise system. He calls this educational process the Great Game of Business. The process is designed to teach all the employees how the business is run, and how employees can relate to their part of the business by means of individual function and financial statements. The game is played by all employees as they follow the action through weekly income statements. The system has some normal as well as not so normal facets:[29]

   1. All employees own stock through an employee stock option plan.

2. Secrecy is cow manure.

3. All employees are trained in how to make money, how to make a profit:
   - They must all be able to read and understand the income statement.
   - Each person knows where he or she shows up in the income statement.
   - The goals are set based on the income statement and this makes the people accountable for their part, their raises, their bonuses.

4. Goals are to improve sales and profits per employee.

The bottom line of this unusual, but not unique, application is that it provides the people with a structure whereby they can support the company. It teaches them what each person has to do to make the company successful. The goals that are established are based on the security of the company: to create jobs and keep people working. Each goal is a must, not a want. The intent is to create a company that will be ongoing 50 years in the future.

More important to John Stack is creating a system that makes everybody aware of the company's strengths and weaknesses, and that forces the weaknesses to be addressed.

BARRIERS TO TQM

Getting quality improvement programs implemented has never been easy. They are contrary to tradition and change. Don't waste time on laggards; plant a lot of seeds, water them well, and the forest will engulf those laggards who waste time trying to slow it down. These laggards will be more convinced from the results of visionary leadership than with what anyone can tell them.

General Dynamics is taking their QIP forward with TQM. Potential barriers to TQM were recently developed during a brainstorming session of the division's TQM coordinators/facilitators.[30] Some of these are listed here:

Communications

- Eliminate corporate policies, procedures, and standard practices that are outdated and redundant.

- Company/division size and multiple locations, makes cross-talk very difficult.
- Communication on TQM—what is it? Desired action and the need for a common vocabulary.
- One-way communication—top down versus bottom up.
- Parallel implementation of TQM in line organization.
- Lack of good communications.
- Fear of failure.
- Lack of teaming on ideas.

Organization

- Engineering domination impacts manufacturing.
- TQM should not change my sandbox.
- Organization not structured to accept TQM process.
- Lack of middle management support.
- Lack of delegation to lower labor grades.
- TQM is program of the year.
- Division management is not committed to TQM—one or two levels.
- Why change?

Attitude

- "Good ol' boy" network breaks down management links.
- Style of crisis management; i.e., reactive versus proactive.
- Division arrogance.
- Attitude: beautiful machines—disposable people—nobody really cares.
- Lack of good planning and philosophy.
- Lack of trust in any new initiative.
- Lack of a sense of urgency.
- Competitiveness within and among departments (individual versus teamwork).

External Influence

- Hourly and management support employees are treated as contract labor.
- Union work rules impact productivity/quality.
- Union management opposes teaming on new approaches; i.e., variability reduction program.
- Local customer not following TQM philosophy.
- "Generation gap"—earned rights versus entitled rights.
- Funding to match verbal commitment—"put your money where your mouth is."
- DoD emphasis versus foreign market participation.
- Management-by-objectives process may be counterproductive.

A PRESIDENT'S CHECKLIST

The simplest way to measure long-term improvement processes is to define the expected activities and then ensure that they are being performed. The Honeywell-developed President (or CEO) checklist can be used to evaluate these process activities, then compare this to the goals that are the outputs of the process-oriented activities.[31] This technique was presented at Juran IMPRO 89, Atlanta, Georgia by Arnold Weimeskirch.

Top Management Leadership

- Has the general manager formed a steering committee consisting of the GM and his or her staff to lead TQM?
- How often do they meet?
- Has the steering committee been trained in TQM?
- Has the steering committee formulated a quality strategy for the division?
- Has the division written a TQM plan that includes specific quality goals and action plans?

Division Needs Assessment

- Has the steering committee evaluated the division's current status (baselined) in quality improvement?
- Has the steering committee identified top priority needs for improvement?

Process and Techniques

- Has the steering committee selected specific improvement projects?
- Does the division utilize formal quality techniques in white-collar, as well as factory, areas? (e.g., SPC, Taguchi, QFD, Concurrent Engineering, etc.)

Measurement and Goals

- Does the division have cross-functional measures for quality improvement?
- Has the division included quality goals in their strategic business plan and compensation reward system?
- Has the division documented quantifiable results from quality improvement?

Culture Change

- Are employees empowered to improve their jobs?

Quality Training

- Does the division have a formal training program in quality improvement that covers all departments?

SUMMARY

So what's different? The world has changed and the leaders of the United States have to lead. In the 1960s, 1970s, and 1980s those with money (and overwhelming nuclear advantage) had power. But in the 1990s and into the year 2000, those with quality will have power, lower costs, a competitive advantage, financing, contracts, jobs, improved standards of living—and will survive in the world economy.

Has success corrupted the American dream? Maybe tarnished, but not corrupted. There is much hope. A recent survey done by Ernst and Young of U.S. leaders shows that there has been productivity and quality improvements in the last five years.[32] The major findings, discussed in *Aviation Week* by Stan Kandero, were (a) there have been major improvements in manufacturing productivity, (b) there have been major improvements in first-time quality, and (c) contractors have been able to reduce costs of major weapon systems.

Great nations average about 200 years of existence from origin to fall. Our United States is now 213 years young; where do we fall on this scale?

- From bondage to spiritual faith.
- From spiritual faith to courage.
- From courage to liberty.
- From liberty to abundance.
- From abundance to selfishness.
- From selfishness to complacency.
- From complacency to apathy.
- From apathy to dependency.
- From dependency to bondage.

Surely, we want to regain that overriding leadership that will retain us at the place in history that we want to remain. We have been slipping.

- From courage to liberty!

EPILOGUE

My son, beware of 'good enough,'
It isn't made of sterling stuff;
It's something anyone can do,
It marks the many from the few,
It has no merit to the eye,
It's something anyone can buy,
It's name is but a sham and bluff,
For it is never 'good enough.'

With 'good enough' the shirkers stop
In every factory and shop;
With 'good enough' the failures rest
And lose to those who give their best;

With 'good enough' the car breaks down
And those of high renown fall down.
My son, remember and be wise,
In 'good enough' disaster lies.

With 'good enough' ships have been wrecked,
The forward march of armies checked,
Great buildings burned and fortunes lost;
Nor can the world compute the cost
In life and money it has paid
Because at 'good enough' we stayed.
Who stops at 'good enough' shall find
Success has left them far behind.

There is no 'good enough' that's short
Of what you can do and you ought.
The flaw which may escape the eye
and temporarily get by.
Shall weaken underneath the strain
And wreck the ship or car or train.
For this is true of men and stuff—
Only the best is 'good enough.'

—Edgar A. Guest
1928

Appendixes

Measurement Parameters   A

FUNCTION	PARAMETER	MEASURE
ALL	Overtime	Overtime/Straight Time
	Indirect Headct	Tot Indirect Headct/Tot Direct Headct
	Nonproductive Time vs Tot Time Avail.	Nonproductive Time/Tot Time Avail.
	Travel Costs	Travel $/Cost of Sales $
	Absenteeism	Tot Hrs Absent/Tot Hrs Sched.
	Indirect Dollars	Tot Indirect $/Tot Direct Dollars
	Sales vs Function Indirect Headct	Sales/VA Sales/Indirect Headct
	Cost Reduction Program	Cost Reduction $/#Employees
	Supervisory Ratio	Tot Employees/Tot Supervisors
	Cost Reduction Program	Cost Reduction $/Cost of Sales
	Dept Costs vs Dept Budgeted Costs	Dept Costs/Dept Budgeted Costs
	Sales vs Direct Headct	Sales/VA Sales/Direct Headct
	No. of People in QC Teams vs Tot Employees	No. of People in QC Teams/Tot Employees
	Sales vs Tot Function Headct	Sales/Tot Function Headct
	Sales/VA Sales vs Time Rept Headct	Sales/VA Sales/Time Rept Headct
	Headct vs No. of Secretaries	Headct/No. of Secretaries
	PBIT vs Employees	PBIT/Employees
	Direct vs Indirect Headct	Direct Headct/Indirect Headct
	Sales/VA Sales vs Tot Headct	Sales/VA Sales/Tot Headct
	Unplanned Absent Hrs vs Tot Hrs	Unplanned Absent Hrs/Tot Hrs
	Indirect Headct vs Direct Headct	Indirect Headct/Direct Headct
	Paper File Reduction	Cum File Drawer & Pgs Transferred to Microfiche
	Overtime	Tot Overtime Hrs/Tot Hrs Worked
	Suggestion Program	Employee Suggestions/Tot Employees
	Earned vs Direct Hrs	Earned Hrs/Direct Hrs
	Direct Labor vs Tot Time Rpt Labor	Direct Labor/Tot Time Rpt Labor
	Hrs on Rej Time Rpts vs Tot Hrs Rpt	Hrs on Rej Time Rpts/Tot Hrs Reported
	Earned Hrs vs Direct Hrs	Earned Hrs/Direct Hrs
	Nonconformance Responsibility	Pct Rej by Responsibility–Supp. Gfe, Planning, Eng, Mfg
	Proposal Responsiveness	Delinquent Proposals/Proposals in Work

FUNCTION	PARAMETER	MEASURE
MARKETING	Proposals	Proposals Won/Proposals Submitted
	No. of Proposals vs No. of Mktg Reps.	No. of Proposals/No. of Mktg Reps.
	Proposal Performance	Orders Booked $/B&P Resources $
	Mktg	Orders Rec $/Mktg Headct
	$ Orders Rec YTD vs $ Orders Planned Ytd	$ Orders Rec YTD/$ Orders Planned YTD
CONTRACTS	Contract Rep. Backlog	Sales Backlog/# Contract Reps.
	$ Orders Rec—Mo/Yr vs No. of Marketeers/Contract Admin.	$ Orders Rec—Mo/Yr/No. of Marketeers/Contract Admin.
	Sales/VA Sales vs Comm. Dept Headct	Sales/VA Sales/Comm. Dept Headct
	No. of Active Contracts vs No. of Contract Admin.	No. of Active Contracts/No. of Contract Admin.
	Sales Proposal $ vs $ Orders Rec	Sales Proposal $/$ Orders Rec
	Contracts	Active Contracts #/Contracts Headct
DATA SYSTEMS	Cptr Aided Graphics Productivity	CAG Prod. Efficiency/Manual Prod Efficiency
	Mrp/Hms Performance/Usage vs Various Mrp/Hms Crit	Mrp/Hms Performance/Usage/Various Mrp/Hms Crit
	On Time Delivery of Crit Cptr	On Time Crit Cptr Rpts/Tot Crit Rpts
	Online Uptime Performance	Sys Avail. During Published Sched. Hrs/Sched. Hrs
	Proj Est Develop. Cost vs Proj Act Develop. Cost	Proj Est Develop. Cost/Proj Act Develop. Cost
	Output Distributed On Time vs Tot Output Distributed	Output Distributed On Time/Tot Output Distributed
	Abnormal Termination of Batch Sys	Batch Abends/Production Cpu Time
	Quality of Deliverable Software	Number of Errors/1000 Bytes of Code
	User Complaints vs Hrs of Usage	User Complaints/Hrs of Usage
	Operations Budget vs IS Budget	Operations Budget/IS Budget
	Out of Service Terminal vs Tot No. of Terminals	Out of Service Terminals/Tot No. of Terminals
	Pgs Printed Per Manhr	No. Pgs Printed/Number of Manhrs
	Abnormal Termination of Online Sys	Online Abends/Online Transactions
	Keypunch Earned Hrs vs Keypunch Act Hrs	Keypunch Earned Hrs/Keypunch Act Hrs
	Jobs Completed vs Jobs Sched.	Jobs Completed/Jobs Sched.

FUNCTION	PARAMETER	MEASURE
	Tot Operations Headct vs IS Headct	Tot Operations Headct/IS Headct
	Trouble Calls Rec vs Unit of Time (Wk, Mo, Etc)	Trouble Calls Rec/Unit of Time (Wk, Mo, Etc)
	Hardware Uptime vs Tot Hardware Time	Hardware Uptime/Tot Hardware Time
	Cadam Errors	Hrs to Correct Cadam Errors/Support Hrs
ENGINEERING	$ Orders Rec vs Serv. Eng Budget	$ Orders Rec/Serv. Eng Budget
	No. of EOCs vs No. of Engineers	No. of EOCs/No. of Engineers
	Eng Rej Rate	Rej/Eng Design Hrs
	Avoidable Eng Changes	Avoidable Eng Chgs/Tot Eng Releases
	Eng Nonconformance $$	Eng Nonconformance $/Tot Nonconformance $
	Eng Obsolescence	Eng Obsolescence $/Tot Mfg $
	Cad Hrs Usage vs Cad Hrs Available	Cad Hrs Usage/Cad Hrs Available
	Operations Budget vs. Serv. Eng Budget	Operations Budget/Serv. Eng Budget
	Bid Hrs vs Est Hrs	Bid Hrs/Est Hrs
	Serv. Eng Budget vs Operations Sales	Serv. Eng Budget/Operations Sales
	Factory Costs vs Prod Eng Costs	Factory Costs/Prod Eng Costs
	No. of Drawings vs Drafting Headct	No. of Drawings/Drafting Headct
	Cost to Prepare Drawings vs No. of Drawings Produced	Cost to Prepare Drawings/No. of Drawings Produced
	Eng Chg Orders Per Drawing	No. of ECOs/No. of Drawings
	Eng Proposal Performance	# Proposals Submitted/# Proposals Won
	Proj with Plans vs Tot Proj	Proj with Plans/Tot Proj
	Eng Bill of Matl Accuracy	No. of Bom Line Items Incorrect/Tot No. of Bom Line Items
	Design to Production Transition Index	# Procurement Problems Resulting in Redesign/# Problem
	No. of ECOs vs Drawings	No. of ECOs/Drawings
	No. Software Instructions vs No. of Software Engineers	No. Software Instructions/No. of Software Engineers

FUNCTION	PARAMETER	MEASURE
	Data Base Use	No. of Times a Cag/Cad D Base Is Used as Basis for Addtl
	Proj Overrun $ vs Tot Proj $	Proj Overrun $/Tot Proj $
	Std Parts in New Releases	Std Parts in New Releases / Tot Parts in New Releases
	Tot Operations Personnel vs Serv. Eng Personnel	Tot Operations Personnel/Serv. Eng Personnel
	Eng Response	Avg Hrs to Respond to Rqst for Eng Action
ESTIMATING	Planned Cost All Programs vs Act Cost All Programs	Planned Cost All Programs/Act Cost All Programs
	Projected Unit Build Cost vs Target Unit Build Cost	Projected Unit Build Cost/Target Unit Build Cost
	Act Hrs/$ vs Est Hrs/$	Act Hrs/$/Est Hrs/$
	Neg. Hrs vs Bid Hrs	Neg. Hrs/Bid Hrs
FACILITIES	Maint Trades Performance	Maint Work Orders Est/Act Hrs Charged to W.O.s
	Bldg Sq Footage vs Maint Cleaning Personnel	Bldg Sq Footage/Maint Cleaning Personnel
	Backlog Hrs on Maint W.O. vs Maint. Headct	Backlog Hrs on Maint W.O./Maint Headct
	Custodial Evaluation Index	Task Points Earned/Tot Possible Points
	Maint Orders Within Est vs Tot Maint Orders	Maint Orders Within Est/Tot Maint Orders
FINANCE	Bookings	Orders Booked $/Month
	Fp Orders with Progress Payments vs Tot No. of Fp Orders	Fp Orders with Progress Payments / Tot No. of Fr Orders
	No. of DD250 Errors vs Tot DD250S Processed	No. of DD250 Errors / Tot DD250S Processed
	Finance Dept Budget vs Sales	Finance Dept Budget/Sales
	Receivables Over 60 Days vs Tot Receivables	Receivables Over 60 Days/Tot Receivables
	Invoices Processed X Std vs Disbursement Audit Hrs	Invoices Processed X Std/Disbursement Audit Hrs
	Order Booking Performance	Value of Goods Booked/Value of Books Planned
	Operations Budget vs Finance Dept Budget	Operations Budget/Finance Dept Budget
	Trade Billed Receivables vs Avg Trade Billed Sales/Day	Trade Billed Receivables/Avg Trade Billed Sales/Day
	Value Added Sales	Sales $/Employee

FUNCTION	PARAMETER	MEASURE
	$ Value of Pricing Proposals vs No. of Pricing People	$ Value of Pricing Proposals/No. of Pricing People
	No. of Pricing Proposals vs No. of Pricing People	No. of Pricing Proposals/No. of Pricing People
	Errors in Data Collection vs Volume of Data Collected	Errors in Data Collection/Volume of Data Collected
	Tot Operations Personnel vs Finance Personnel	Tot Operations Personnel/Finance Personnel
	Invoice Collections	Invoice $ Older than 30 Days/Accts Rec $
	Sales/VA Sales vs Finance Personnel	Sales/VA Sales/Finance Personnel
	Net Assets Sales vs Sales	Net Assets Sales/Sales
	Past Due Receivables	Receivables Past Due/Receivables Billed
	Act Burden Rate vs Planned Burden Rate	Act Burden Rate/Planned Burden Rate
	Incomplete Cost Std vs Tot Cost Std	Incomplete Cost Std/Tot Cost Std
	Invoicing Errors vs Invoices Processed	Invoicing Errors/Invoices Processed
	Journal Voucher Errors	Vouchers in Error/Tot Vouchers
GENERAL MANAGER	Operations Headct vs Dept Headct	Operations Headct/Dept Headct
	Cust. Deficiency Rpts	Number Rpts/Plant Population
	Assets vs Employees	Assets/Employees
	Operations Sales/VA Sales vs Dept Headct	Operations Sales/VA Sales/Dept Headct
	Cust. Satisfaction Index	
	Profit vs Employees	Profit/Employees
	Sales vs Assets	Sales/Assets
	Nonconformance $ Impact on Profit	Nonconformance $/Profit $
INDUSTRIAL RELATIONS	Workers Compensation Costs vs Tot Hrs Worked	Workers Compensation Costs/Tot Hrs Worked
	Employees Terminating vs Tot Employees	Employees Terminating/Tot Employees
	Chg Notices Processed vs No. of Compensation Clericals	Chg Notices Processed/No. of Compensation Clericals
	No. of People Interviewed & Hired vs No. of People Interviewed	No. of People Interviewed & Hired/No. of People Interviewed

FUNCTION	PARAMETER	MEASURE
	Insurance Claims Processed vs No. of Insurance Claim Clerks	Insurance Claims Processed Insurance/No. of Claim Clerks
	Elapsed Time of Unprocessed ECRs vs No. of Unprocessed ECRs	Elapsed Time of Unprocessed ECRs/No. of Unprocessed ECRs
	No. of Chg Notice Errors vs Tot Chg Notices	No. of Chg Notice Errors/Tot Chg Notices
	No. Personnel Tranfers vs Headct	No. Personnel Tranfers/Headct
	Operations Support vs Employees Rel Budget	Operations Support/Employees Rel Budget
	Sales/VA Sales vs Employees Rel Headct	Sales/VA Sales/Employees Rel Headct
	Sales/VA Sales vs IS Headct	Sales/VA Sales/IS Headct
	No. of Personnel Transfers vs Headvt	No. of Personnel Transfers/Headct
	Avg Cost Per Proff. Hire	Tot Recruit. & Reloc. Cost/No. of Proff. Hires
	Offers Made vs Offers Accepted	Offers Made/Offers Accepted
	Tot Operations Headct vs Employees Rel Headct	Tot Operations Headct/Employees Rel Headct
LOGISTICS	Mod Kit Sched. Performance	Act Deliveries/Sched. Deliveries
	Mod Kit Accpt Rate	Tot Accpt/Tot Inspected
	Support Equip Accpt Rate	Tot Accpt/Tot Inspected
	Specific Prog Logistics Orders vs Specific Prog Nonlogistics Order	Specific Prog Logistics Orders/Specific Prog Nonlogistics Orders
	Maint Costs/Flt Hr vs Target Cost	Maint Costs/Flt Hr/Target Cost
	Qty of Spares Delivered vs Qty of Spares to Be Delivered Per Contract	Qty of Spares Delivered/Qty of Spares to Be Delivered Per Contract
	Units In-House for Repair vs Units Installed	Units In-House For Repair/Units Installed
	Sales/VA Sales vs Serv Eng Headct	Sales/VA Sales/Serv Eng Headct
	No. of Programs Where PVWA > Actuals vs No. of Programs	No. of Programs Where PVWA > Actuals/No. of Programs
	Supt Equip Sched. Performance	Act Deliveries/Sched. Deliveries
	Avg Grade Level of Field Engineers vs Avg Grade Level of Ideal Work Force	Avg Grade Level of Field Engineers/Avg Grade Level of Ideal Work Force
	Tech Order Sched. Performance	Act Deliveries/Sched. Deliveries

FUNCTION	PARAMETER	MEASURE
	Avg Maint Down Time of Gyros vs Selected Repair Target (Days)	Avg Maint Down Time of Gyros/Selected Repair Target (Days)
	Service Rpts	Service Rpts Answered Ontime/Service Rpts Due
	Tech Order Error Rate	Tech Order Errors / Tech Order Pgs
	Orders for Logistics Services vs Tot Orders	Orders for Logistics Services/Tot Orders
	Spares Sched. Performance	Act Deliveries / Sched. Deliveries
	Sales/VA Sales vs Logistics Headct	Sales/VA Sales/Logistics Headct
	Spares Acceptance Rate	Tot Accpt/Tot Inspected
MATERIAL	Fixed Price Cost of Sales vs Gross Net Inventory	Fixed Price Cost of Sales/Gross Net Inventory
	No. of P.O.s Placed vs Purchasing Dept Headct	No. of P.O.s Placed/Purchasing Dept Headct
	GFE Nonconformance Cost	Tot Nonconformance $ on GFAE/Tot Mfg Labor $
	Tot Operations Headct vs Purchasing Dept Headct	Tot Operations Headct/Purchasing Dept Headct
	Inventory	Gross Inventory/Sales $
	$ Amt of Purchases vs Purchasing Dept Headct	$ Amt of Purchases/Purchasing Dept Headct
	Procured Material Accpt Rate	# Lots Accpt/# Lots Inspected
	Matl Proposal Records Rec vs Matl Proposal Records Completed	Matl Proposal Records Rec/Matl Proposal Records Completed
	Kit Accuracy	No. of Kits Without Discrep./Tot No. of Kits Inspected
	Cost Per P.O.	Purchasing Edpt Budget/# P.O. Placed
	MRP Product Structure Accuracy	No. of Product Structures With No Errors/Tot No. of Product Structures Revised
	Inventory Accuracy	Inventory Items within Tolerance/Inventory Items Check
	No. of MPRs Returned on Time vs No. of MPRs Returned	No. of MPRs Returned On Time/No. of MPRs Returned
	Work In Process Inventory Turns	Work in Process Inventory Value/Fp Inventory Cost of Sales Less Repair
	Vendor Delivery to Promise	No. of On Time Vendor Delivery/No. of Tot Vendor Deliveries

FUNCTION	PARAMETER	MEASURE
	$ Amt of Purchases vs Purchasing Dept Budget	$ Amt of Purchases/Purchasing Dept Budget
	Matl Dock to Stock Flow Time	No. of Matl Lots to Stock on Time/No. of Tot Matl
	Incoming Matl Lots Accepted vs Incoming Matl Lots	Incoming Matl Lots Accpt/Incoming Matl Lots
	Sales/VA Sales vs Procurement Dept Headct	Sales/VA Sales/Procurement Dept Headct
	Purchased Items	$ Parts Accpt/$ Parts Rec
	Other Losses	Other Matl Loss $/Tot Mfg $
	P.O. Errors vs P.O. Audited	P.O. Errors/P.O. Audited
	Est Savings on Orders Placed vs $ Value of Orders Placed	Est Savings on Orders Placed/$ Value of Orders Placed
	Receiving Turnaround	Receipts Processed within 24 Hrs/Tot Dock Receipts
	On Time Deliveries	On Time Issues/Production Demands
OFFICE SERVICES	Reproduction Costs vs No. of Pgs Produced	Reproduction Costs/No. of Pgs Produced
	Viewgraphs Redone vs Tot Viewgraphs Produced	Viewgraphs Redone/Tot Viewgraphs Produced
	Operations Headct vs Comm. Dept Headct	Operations Headct/Comm. Dept Headct
	Cost of Viewgraph Chgs vs Tot Graphics Cost	Cost of Viewgraph Chgs/Tot Graphics Cost
PRODUCTION	Scrap	(Scrap Hrs/Direct Labor Hrs) & (Scrap Matl $/Tot Matl $)
	Scrap/Rework	Scrap & Rework $/Sales
	Nonconformance Costs	Tot Nonconformance $/Tot Mfg $
	Flight Discrep. Per Flight	Avg No. Flight Discrep./Number of Flights
	Rework/Repair Labor	Rework & Repair Labor $/Tot Mfg Labor $
	Scrap Material	Scrap Material $/Tot Material $
	Zero Defect Program	Zero Discrepant Products Delivered/Tot Mfg
	Scrap Labor	Scrap Labor $/Tot Mfg Labor $
	Scrap/Rework/Repair Processing Costs	SRR Processing Support $/Tot Mfg Labor $
	Rej Per Parts Mfg	Tot Parts Rej During Mfg/Parts Mfg
	Warranty Repair Costs vs Sales	Warranty Repair Costs / Sales
	Set-up vs Earned	Set-up Hrs / Earned Hrs
	Rework $ Scrap $	Rework $ Scrap $/Mfg Hr

FUNCTION	PARAMETER	MEASURE
	Rework Hrs Per Printed Wiring Assy	Rework Hrs/Printed Wiring Assys Shipped
	Production Output to Plan	Production Output parts/plan no. part s
	Rework & Repair Rate	Rework & Repair $/Std Labor $
	Flight Inspection Program	Customer Flight Disc Per Ac/Contractor Flight Disc Per
	Reflight Cost	Aircraft Relight Cost/No. of Aircraft
	Nonconformance Cost Per Ship	Tot Nonconformance Dollars/Equivalent Ship Set
	Flight Inspection	No. Flights to Acceptance/No. of Aircraft
	Backlog of Deviant Matl	Trend of Swell Time in Rework Cycle
	DD250 Performance	Avg Hrs Between Last Inspection/Flt to DD250
	Top 5 Defects	List Defects
	Direct vs Std Hrs	Direct Hrs/Std Hrs
	Std Repairs	No. Std Repairs/1000 Mfg Hrs
	Low Dollar Scrap	Tot Low Dollar Scrap $/Tot Mfg $
	Flight Aborts	Tot Flight Aborts/No. Flight Attempts
	Retest Ratio	Unit Retest Hrs/Unit Test Hrs
	Labor Performance vs Plan	Act Hrs Per Equivalent Unit/Planned Hrs Per Equivalent Unit
	Scrap Dollars Per Equivalent Unit	Scrap Dollars/Equivalent Units Produced
	Rework $ Scrap $	Rework $ Scrap $/Sales $
	Rej Processing Labor Index	Relates to Processing Labor/No. of Rej
	Prod Hrly Headct vs Prod Control Headct	Prod Hrly Headct/Prod Control Headct
	Product Build & Supt Hrs vs Equivalent Unit	Product Build & Supt Hrs/Equivalent Unit
	Units Sched. vs Units Produced	Units Sched./Units Produced
	Acceptance Rate	No. of Units Accpt/No. of Units Inspected
	Direct Labor $ vs Std Hrs	Direct Labor $ Hrs/Std Hrs
	Scrap $	Scrap $/Sales $
	Major Rej Costs	Rej Documents Requiring Corrective Action/Tot Rej $

FUNCTION	PARAMETER	MEASURE
PRODUCTION	Rework $	Rework $/Mfg Hr
	Rework $ Scrap Labor	Rework $ Scrap Labor/Mfg Labor
	Wait Time Hrs vs Direct Labor Hrs	Wait Time Hrs/Direct Labor Hrs
	Hrs on Labor Ticket Rej vs Tot Hrs Rept	Hrs on Labor Ticket Rej/Tot Hrs Rept
	Defects Per Transformer	Defects/# Transformers Inspected
	Prod Build Hrs on Layouts vs Prod Build Hrs	Prod Build Hrs on Layouts/Prod Build Hrs
	Customer Accpt Lots vs Lots Submitted	Customer Accpt Lots/Lots Submitted
	Tot Prod. Hrs vs Direct Earned Hrs	Tot Prod. Hrs vs/Direct Earned Hrs
	No. of Defects vs No. of Units Inspected	No. of Defects/No. of Units Inspected
	Support Cost Per Operator	Support Cost/#Production Operators
	Inventory Shortage vs Inventory Additions	Inventory Shortage/Inventory Additions
	Production Support Costs vs Prod LBM	Prod. SPT Costs/Prod LBM Costs
	Cost of Sales vs Gross Inventory	Cost of Sales/Gross Inventory
	Prod SPT Costs vs Prod LBM Costs	Prod SPT Costs/Prod LBM Costs
	Salvage vs Direct Hrs	Salvage Hrs/Direct Hrs
	Scrap $	Scrap $/Mfg Hr
	Indirect vs Direct Hrs	Indirect Hrs/Direct Hrs
	Scrap Costs vs LBM Additions	Scrap Costs/LBM Additions
	Product Delivery	Avg Days Past Due
	Hrs Per Equivalent Unit	(Fab+Assy+Test+Insp+Supt Hrs)/Equivalent Units Produced
	Production Control Support Ration	Production Control Direct Hrs/Fab+Assy+Test+Insp+Supt Hrs
	Rej Per Hr	No. Rej Documents/1000 Manhours
	Prod Hrly Headct vs Prod Eng Headct	Prod Hrly Headct/Prod Eng Headct
	Rework/Direct Labor Ratio	Rework Direct Labor/Tot Direct Labor
	Completed Kits	Completed Kits Issued/Tot Kits Issued
	Mk 46 Prod. Productivity Index	Direct Labor Hrs X Performance/Tot Hrs

FUNCTION	PARAMETER	MEASURE
	Major Rej Documents	Rej Documents Requiring Corrective Action/Tot Rej Documents
	Scrap Rate	Scrap Labor $ Std Labor $
	Matl Review Documents	Matl Review Documents Per 1000 Manhrs
	Rework $	Rework $/Sales $
	Equipment Cost Savings	Savings vs Equipment Cost & 2.5 Year Payback
	Equipment Acquisition	Service Rqsts Behind Sched./Rqsts Ahead of Sched.
	First Time Yield (FAB)	Parts Accept First Time/Tot Parts Presented
	Rework/Repair	Rework & Repair Hrs/Direct Mfg Lab Hrs
	Equipment Cost	Equipment Cost/Cost of Sales
PROGRAM OFFICE	RFG Response	(Price/Tech) on Time vs Due Date
	Milestones Completed ltd vs Milestones Sched. ltd	Milestones Completed ltd/Milestones Sched. ltd
	Warranty Costs	Dollars Per Mo/% to Hardware Sales
	No. of Key Performance Specs Met vs Tot No. of Key Performance Specs	No. of Key Perf. Specs Met/Tot No. of Key Perf. Specs
	COD ECPs	Cod ECPs/Tot ECPs
	Operational Readiness	Mc & Fmc Aircraft/Aircraft In Fleet
	Customer Complaints	Customer Complaints Per 1000 Manhrs
	Deviations & Waivers	Deviations & Waivers / Delivered End Items
QUALITY ASSURANCE	Appraisal Costs vs COQ	Appraisal Costs/COQ
	Act Burden Rate vs Planned Burden Rate	Act Burden Rate / Planned Burden Rate
	Failure Costs vs COQ	Failure Costs/COQ
	Quality Dept Hrs vs Prod Hrs	Quality Dept Hrs/Prod Hrs
	Tot Operating Headct vs Quality Dept Headct	Tot Operating Headct/Quality Dept Headct
	End Item Inspection Discrepancies	Customer Initiated/Contractor Initiated
	Matl Surveys	Tot Surveys Conducted/Tot End Items Mfg
	Age of Open Rejections	Rej Open Over 120 Days Per Month/Rej Initiated Each Month

FUNCTION	PARAMETER	MEASURE
	Matl Review Documents	Matl Review Rejection Documents/Tot Rej Documents
	COQ vs Cost of Sales	COQ/COS
	COQ	Cost of Inspected Scrap, Rework Support Services
	Matl Lots Inspected vs Rec Inspected Headct	Matl Lots Inspected/Rec. Inspected Headct
	Sales/VA Sales vs Product Assurance Headct	Sales/VA Sales/Product Assurance Headct
	Operations Budget vs Quality Dept Budget	Operations Budget/Quality Dept Budget
	Calibration Manhrs Per Unit	Calibration Manhrs/Units Calibrated
	No. of DD250 Errors vs Tot DD250's Processed	No. of DD250 Errors/Tot DD250's Processed
	Errors on Inspection Procedures vs Inspected Procedures Issued	Errors on Inspection Procedures/Inspected Procedures Issued
	QE Supt Cost vs Prod Lbm Costs	QE Supt Cost/Prod Lbm Costs
	Prevention Costs vs COQ	Prevention Costs/COQ
	Major Rejection Costs	Rej $ Requiring Corrective Action/Tot Rej $
	Could Not Duplicate	Number of Units Tested CND/Tot Tested Units Rejected
	Tot Rec Inspected Hrs vs Lots Rec	Tot Rec Inspected Hrs/Lots Rec
	Quality Indirect Hrs vs Tot Quality Hrs	Quality Indirect Hrs Tot Quality Hrs
	Production Earned Hrs vs Quality Eng Supt Hrs	Production Earned Hrs/Quality Eng Supt Hrs
	Major Rej	Major Rej Documents/Direct Labor Hrs
	DD250 Errors	Erroneous DD250S/Tot DD250S
	Inspection Escapes	Out-of-Dept Rej/Tot Inspections
SAFETY	Lost Time for Injuries vs Tot Hrs Worked	Lost Time for Injuries/Tot Hrs Worked
VENDOR	Supplier Nonconformance Costs	Tot Nonconformance $ on Supplier Items/Tot Mfg Labor $
	Vendor Performance	Lots Defective
	Vendor Performance	On Time
	Warranty Returns	Avg Turnaround Time in Days

1990 Application Guidelines

Malcolm Baldrige
National Quality Award

"The improvement
of quality in
products and the
improvement of
quality in service —
these are national
priorities as
never before."

George Bush

"The success of the
Malcolm Baldrige
National Quality Award
has demonstrated
that government and
industry, working together,
can foster excellence."

Robert Mosbacher
Secretary of Commerce

EXAMINATION CATEGORIES, ITEMS, AND POINT VALUES

Malcolm Baldrige National Quality Award

1990 Examination Categories/Items	Maximum Points
1.0 Leadership	100
1.1 Senior Executive Leadership	30
1.2 Quality Values	20
1.3 Management for Quality	30
1.4 Public Responsibility	20
2.0 Information and Analysis	60
2.1 Scope and Management of Quality Data and Information	35
2.2 Analysis of Quality Data and Information	25
3.0 Strategic Quality Planning	90
3.1 Strategic Quality Planning Process	40
3.2 Quality Leadership Indicators in Planning	25
3.3 Quality Priorities	25
4.0 Human Resource Utilization	150
4.1 Human Resource Management	30
4.2 Employee Involvement	40
4.3 Quality Education and Training	40
4.4 Employee Recognition and Performance Measurement	20
4.5 Employee Well-Being and Morale	20
5.0 Quality Assurance of Products and Services	150
5.1 Design and Introduction of Quality Products and Services	30
5.2 Process and Quality Control	25
5.3 Continuous Improvement of Processes, Products and Services	25
5.4 Quality Assessment	15
5.5 Documentation	10
5.6 Quality Assurance, Quality Assessment and Quality Improvement of Support Services and Business Processes	25
5.7 Quality Assurance, Quality Assessment and Quality Improvement of Suppliers	20
6.0 Quality Results	150
6.1 Quality of Products and Services	50
6.2 Comparison of Quality Results	35
6.3 Business Process, Operational and Support Service Quality Improvement	35
6.4 Supplier Quality Improvement	30
7.0 Customer Satisfaction	300
7.1 Knowledge of Customer Requirements and Expectations	50
7.2 Customer Relationship Management	30
7.3 Customer Service Standards	20
7.4 Commitment to Customers	20
7.5 Complaint Resolution for Quality Improvement	30
7.6 Customer Satisfaction Determination	50
7.7 Customer Satisfaction Results	50
7.8 Customer Satisfaction Comparison	50
TOTAL POINTS	1000

1990 EXAMINATION

1.0 Leadership (100 pts.)

The **Leadership** category examines how the senior executives create and sustain a clear and visible quality value system along with a supporting management system to guide all activities of the company toward quality excellence. Also examined are the senior executives' and the company's quality leadership in the external community and how the company integrates its public responsibilities with its quality values and practices.

1.1 Senior Executive Leadership (30 pts.)   Describe the senior executives' leadership, personal involvement, and visibility in developing and maintaining an environment for quality excellence.

Areas to Address

   a. senior executives' leadership and personal involvement in quality-related activities such as goal setting, planning, review of quality plans and progress, teams, giving and receiving education and training, recognition of employees, learning about the quality of domestic and international competitors, and meeting with customers and suppliers

   b. senior executives' approach to building the quality values into the leadership process of the company

   c. senior executives' communication, access and contact within the company

   d. senior executives' leadership and communication of quality excellence outside the company to groups such as national, trade, business, professional and community organizations, and schools

Note: *The term* **senior executives** *refers to the highest ranking official of the organization applying for the Award and those reporting directly to that official.*

1.2 Quality Values (20 pts.)   Describe the company's quality values, how they are projected in a consistent manner, and how adoption of the values throughout the company is assessed and reinforced.

Areas to Address

   a. brief summary of the content of policy, mission or guidelines that demonstrate the company's quality values

b. company's communications activities and plans to project the values throughout the company

c. recent or current actions that demonstrate the importance of the quality values with respect to other business considerations, such as short-term profits and schedules

d. how the company evaluates the extent to which the quality values have been adopted throughout the company, such as through surveys, interviews or other means, and how employee acceptance is reinforced

1.3 Management for Quality (30 pts.)   Describe how the company integrates its quality values into day-to-day management of all units.

Areas to Address

a. key strategies for involving all levels of management and supervision in quality, and principal roles and responsibilities at each level

b. key strategies to promote cooperation among managers and supervisors at all levels such as through use of interunit teams or internal customer/supplier techniques

c. types, frequency and content of company reviews of the status of quality plans, and types of actions taken to assist units not performing according to plans

d. how management assesses the effectiveness of its approaches and improves or changes its approaches to integrating quality values into day-to-day management

e. key indicators of involvement of all levels of management and of effective cooperation among managers

1.4 Public Responsibility (20 pts.)   Describe how the company extends its quality leadership to the external community and integrates its responsibilities to the public for health, safety, environmental protection, and ethical business practice into its quality policies and activities.

Areas to Address

a. promoting quality awareness and sharing with external groups such as community, business, trade, school and government organizations

b. encouraging employee leadership and involvement in quality activities of professional, local, state, national, trade, business and education groups and in industry, national and international standards activities

c. full integration of business ethics, public health and safety, environmental protection, waste management and other regulatory requirements into overall quality leadership policies, systems and continuous improvement objectives

2.0 Information and Analysis (60 pts.)

The *Information and Analysis* category examines the scope, validity, use, and management of data and information that underlie the company's total quality management system. Also examined is the adequacy of the data and information to support a responsive prevention approach to quality based upon "management by fact."

2.1 Scope and Management of Quality Data and Information (35 pts.) Describe the company's base of data and information used for planning, management, and evaluation of quality, and how data and information reliability, timeliness, and access are assured.

Areas to Address

a. criteria for selecting items to be included in the quality-related data and information base

b. scope and types of data: customers; internal operations and processes; employee-related; safety, health and other regulatory; competitive and benchmark data; quality results; supplier quality; and other

c. processes and technologies the company uses to ensure validity, consistency, standardization, review, update and timely access throughout the company

Note: *The purpose of this Item is to permit the applicant to demonstrate the* breadth and depth *of the data assembled as part of its total quality management effort. Applicants should give brief descriptions of the types of data under major headings such as "employees" and subheadings such as "education and training," "teams," and "recognition." Under each subheading, give a brief description of the data and information. Actual data should not be reported in this Item. Such data are requested in other Examination Items.*

2.2 Analysis of Quality Data and Information (25 pts.) Describe how data and information are analyzed to support the company's key quality leadership objectives in a timely manner.

Areas to Address

    a. principal types of analysis performed such as determination of trends, projections of quality improvements that should result from changes in practice or technology, evaluation of the performance of key systems, and assessment of long-term performance of products

    b. how analysis supports key objectives and functions such as planning, day-to-day quality improvement activities, policy development, human resource strategy development, and management review of quality

    c. steps taken and plans to shorten the cycle of data gathering, analysis, and access to improve support of company quality objectives

    d. how analysis leads to changes in types of data collected, improved reliability of data, and improved analytical capabilities

3.0 Strategic Quality Planning (90 pts.)

The **Strategic Quality Planning** category examines the company's planning process for retaining or achieving quality leadership and how the company integrates quality improvement planning into overall business planning. Also examined are the company's short-term and longer-term priorities to achieve and/or sustain a quality leadership position.

    3.1 Strategic Quality Planning Process (40 pts.)   Describe the company's strategic quality planning process for short-term (1–2 years) and longer-term (3–5 years or more) quality leadership and customer satisfaction.

Areas to Address

    a. how strategic quality plans are developed and how they are integrated with overall business planning

    b. principal types of data, information and analysis used in planning and feasibility evaluation such as customer requirements, process capabilities, competitive and benchmark data, and supplier data

    c. principal roles competitive and benchmark data play in determining projected or potential improvements in quality, closing quality gaps, or exceeding competitors' capabilities

d. how employees, suppliers, and customers contribute to planning

e. how key requirements such as new technology, employee education and training, and improvements in supplier quality are determined

f. how plans are implemented such as through priority initiatives or projects; how resources are committed for key requirements such as capital expenditures and training; and how specific requirements are deployed to all work units and to suppliers

g. how the planning process is evaluated and improved

3.2 Quality Leadership Indicators in Planning (25 pts.)   Describe the company's approach to selecting quality-related competitive comparisons and world-class benchmarks to support strategic quality planning.

Areas to Address

a. criteria the company uses for selecting competitive comparisons and benchmarks: what areas to benchmark and with whom to compare

b. current sources of competitive and benchmark data including company and independent testing

c. current actions and plans to change the scope of competitive and benchmark data, to seek new or additional sources of such data, or to change the basis for selection

3.3 Quality Priorities (25 pts.)   Summarize the company's principal quality priorities and plans for the short term (1−2 years) and longer term (3−5 years or more).

Areas to Address

a. principal short-term and longer-term priorities and their relationship to the company's leadership objectives

b. resources committed to plans for education and training, technology and other key requirements

c. how the company will ensure that suppliers are able to meet its quality requirements

d. projection of major changes in the company's competitive quality position based upon implementation of the plan

4.0 Human Resource Utilization (150 pts.)

The *Human Resource Utilization* category examines the effectiveness of the company's efforts to develop and realize the full potential of the work force, including management, and to maintain an environment conducive to full participation, quality leadership, and personal and organizational growth.

4.1 Human Resource Management (30 pts.) Describe how the company's human resource plans support its quality leadership objectives; summarize principal short-term (1–2 years) and longer-term (3–5 years or more) priorities.

Areas to Address

a. how the company integrates its human resource plans with the quality requirements of business plans

b. key strategies for increasing the involvement, effectiveness and productivity of all categories of employees, including hourly, bargaining unit and contract employees, and managers

c. principal human resource priorities for the short term and longer term and how they relate to the company's quality priorities

d. how the company uses its overall employee-related data to evaluate and improve its human resource management, strategies, practices and plans

Note: *Key strategies might include one or more of the following: mechanisms for promoting cooperation such as internal customer/supplier techniques or other internal partnerships; initiatives to promote labor-management cooperation such as partnerships with unions; creation or modifications in recognition systems; mechanisms for increasing or broadening employee responsibilities; and education and training initiatives. They might also include developing partnerships with educational institutions to develop employees and to help ensure the future supply of well-prepared employees.*

4.2 Employee Involvement (40 pts.) Describe the means available for all employees to contribute effectively to the company's quality objectives; summarize trends in involvement.

Areas to Address

a. approaches to group participation such as teams: within functional units; between functional units; and involving suppliers and customers

b. other opportunities for employees to contribute, such as through suggestion systems or hotlines, and how and when the company gives feedback

c. approaches to enhanced employee authority to act (empowerment) such as when quality standards may be compromised; means for encouraging employee innovation; and means for increasing employee responsibilities

d. trends in key indicators of involvement, empowerment, and innovation for all categories of employees

e. principal means the company uses to evaluate the extent and effectiveness of involvement of categories of employees

4.3 Quality Education and Training (40 pts.) Describe how the company decides what quality education and training is needed by employees and how it utilizes the knowledge and skills acquired; summarize the types of quality education and training received by employees in all employee categories.

Areas to Address

a. approach and rationale for deciding what quality education and training, such as training in statistical and other quantitative problem solving methods, is needed by different categories of employees

b. how the company provides on-job reinforcement of the knowledge and skills acquired in education and training

c. summary and trends in types of quality education and training received by each employee category. The summary and trends may address quality orientation of new employees, percent of employees receiving education and training in each category, quality education and training costs per employee, and average hours of quality education and training annually per employee.

d. indicators of effectiveness of the company's education and training activities and how the indicators are used to improve these activities

4.4 Employee Recognition and Performance Measurement (20 pts.) Describe how the company's recognition and performance measurement processes support quality improvement; summarize trends in recognition.

Areas to Address

a. key strategies for encouraging contributions to quality including recognition of individuals and groups; how balance is achieved—between individual and group recognition and between individual and group performance—to ensure effective support for company quality improvement efforts

b. how recognition and performance measures reinforce quality relative to other business considerations such as quantity; how employees are involved in the development of measures

c. summary and trends in recognition of individuals and groups, by employee category, for contributions to quality improvement

d. how the company evaluates the effectiveness of its recognition and performance measurement systems, including soliciting feedback from employees, to improve its strategies and methods

4.5 Employee Well-Being and Morale (20 pts.) Describe how the company safeguards the health and safety of employees, ensures comfort and physical protection, and maintains a supportive work environment; summarize trends in employee well-being and morale.

Areas to Address

a. how well-being and morale factors such as health, safety, satisfaction, and ergonomics are included in quality improvement activities

b. analysis of underlying causes of accidents, work-related health problems, and dissatisfaction, for elimination of adverse conditions

c. mobility, flexibility and retraining in job assignments to support employee development and/or to accommodate changes in technology, improved productivity or changes in work processes

d. special services, facilities and opportunities the company makes available to support employees. These might include one or more of the following: counseling, assistance, recreational or cultural, and non-work-related education

e. how employee satisfaction is determined, evaluated and used in quality improvement

f. trends in key indicators of well-being and morale such as safety, absenteeism, turnover, satisfaction, grievances, strikes and worker compensation. Explain adverse indicators and how problems were resolved or current status. Compare most significant indicators with those of industry averages and industry leaders.

5.0 Quality Assurance of Products and Services (150 pts.)

The *Quality Assurance of Products and Services* category examines the systematic approaches used by the company for total quality control of goods and services based primarily upon process design and control, including control of procured materials, parts and services. Also examined is the integration of quality control with continuous quality improvement.

5.1 Design and Introduction of Quality Products and Services (30 pts.)   Describe how new or improved products and services are designed and introduced to meet or exceed customer requirements and how processes are designed to deliver according to the requirements.

Areas to Address

a. conversion of customer needs and expectations into product and process requirements and/or service quality standards

b. methods and their application for assuring quality in the design, development and validation stages; methods of testing and evaluating products, processes, and services before introduction, including review of designs for feasibility and assessment of key factors in production and use

c. detailed control plan: (1) selecting and setting key process characteristics to be controlled and how they are to be controlled, and (2) service process and delivery plan including selection of key characteristics to be controlled and how they are to be controlled

d. steps taken in design to minimize introduction time

Notes: *(1) In responding to this Item, applicants should interpret product and service characteristics broadly. Most companies have both product and service characteristics to consider.*

(2) Depending on their type of business, applicants need to consider many factors in product and service design including health, safety, long-term performance, measurement capability, process capability, and supplier capability. Applicant responses should reflect the requirements of the products and services they deliver.

5.2 Process and Quality Control (25 pts.) Describe how the processes which produce the company's products and services are controlled and how the company assures that products and services meet design plans or specifications.

Areas to Address

a. principal approaches the company uses to ensure that processes which produce products and services are adequately controlled

b. principal approaches the company uses routinely to ensure that products and services meet design plans or specifications

c. method for assuring that measurement quality is adequate to evaluate products, processes and services within the limits established in control plans

d. principal approaches to identify root causes of process upsets

e. principal approaches to the design of the measures to correct process upsets, and methods of verifying that the measures produce the predicted results and are effectively utilized in all appropriate units of the company

f. principal approaches of the company to use the information obtained from process and quality control for prevention and quality improvement

Note: *For manufacturing and service companies with measurement requirements, it is necessary to demonstrate that measurement accuracy and precision meet process and product requirements (measurement quality assurance). For physical, chemical and engineering measurements, indicate approaches for ensuring that measurements are traceable to national standards through calibrations, reference materials or other means.*

5.3 Continuous Improvement of Processes, Products and Services (25 pts.) Describe how products and services are continuously improved through optimization and improvement of processes.

Areas to Address

a. principal approaches to identify opportunities for continuous improvement of processes, including reductions in response times: evaluation of all process steps; development and assessment of alternative processes; evaluation of new or improved technology; use of competitive and benchmark data

b. methods of process optimization such as controlled experiments

c. method for verifying that improvements produce the predicted results

d. method of integrating continuous improvement with daily operations and routine process and quality control and of ensuring effective integration by all appropriate units of the company

5.4 Quality Assessment (15 pts.) Describe how the company assesses the quality of products, processes, services and quality practices.

Areas to Address

a. principal approaches the company uses to assess quality, quality systems and quality practices such as systems audits, product audits and service audits. Briefly describe the approaches and how the validity of assessment tools is assured.

b. types and frequencies of assessments and who conducts them: the company, customers, government or other

c. how assessment findings are translated into improvements such as in processes, practices, training and supplier requirements

d. method for verifying that improvements are made and that they are producing the predicted results

5.5 Documentation (10 pts.) Describe documentation and other modes of "knowledge preservation" and transfer to support quality assurance, assessment and improvement.

Areas to Address

a. documentation system supporting quality assurance, assessment and improvement; types of documents and types of activities covered; and how documents are used such as in standardization, orientation of new employees, and training

b. timely update to keep pace with changes in technology, practice and quality improvement; disposal of obsolete documents

c. company efforts to improve responsiveness and access of the documentation system such as through use of computers and networks

5.6 Quality Assurance, Quality Assessment and Quality Improvement of Support Services and Business Processes (25 pts.) Describe how the quality of support services and business processes is assured, assessed and improved.

Areas to Address

a. how the quality of support services and business processes is assured such as through process and quality control and quality assessment; how and how often quality is assessed through audits, reviews or other means

b. how support services and business processes are continuously improved

c. current strategies, efforts and plans to increase and improve the participation of support services in quality activities

Notes: *(1) Examples of support services might include finance and accounting, software services, sales, marketing, information services, purchasing, personnel, legal services, maintenance, plant and facilities management, research and development, and secretarial and other administrative services.*

(2) The purpose of this Item is to permit applicants to highlight separately the quality assurance, quality assessment and quality improvement activities for functions that support the primary processes through which products and services are produced. Together, Items 5.1, 5.2, 5.3, 5.4, 5.5, 5.6 and 5.7 should cover all operations, processes and activities of all work units. However, the selection of support services and business processes for inclusion in this Item depends on the type of business and quality system, and should be made by the applicant.

5.7 Quality Assurance, Quality Assessment and Quality Improvement of Suppliers (20 pts.) Describe how the quality of materials, components, and services furnished by other businesses is assured, assessed and improved.

Areas to Address

a. process used to assure that the company's quality requirements are being met by suppliers by means such as audits, inspections, certification and testing

b. strategy and current efforts to improve the quality and responsiveness of suppliers, such as through partnerships, training, incentives and recognition, and to improve supplier selection

Note: *The term supplier refers to external providers of goods and services.*

6.0 Quality Results (150 pts.)

The *Quality Results* category examines quality levels and quality improvement based upon objective measures derived from analysis of customer requirements and expectations and from analysis of business operations. Also examined are current quality levels in relation to those of competing firms.

6.1 Quality of Products and Services (50 pts.) Summarize trends in quality improvement based upon key product and service quality measures derived from customer needs and expectations.

Areas to Address

a. summarize trends in key product and service quality measures

b. explain adverse trends and outline what steps the company has taken or plans to take to prevent recurrence

Note: *Key product and service quality measures are the set of principal measurable characteristics of products and services, including delivery and after-sales services, which, taken together, best represent the* <u>factors that predict customer satisfaction and quality in customer use.</u> *Examples include measures of accuracy, reliability, timeliness, performance, behavior, delivery, documentation and appearance. Customer satisfaction or other customer data should not be included in responses to this Item.*

6.2 Comparison of Quality Results (35 pts.) Compare the company's current quality levels with industry averages, industry leaders and world leaders, based upon the key product and service quality measures reported in Item 6.1.

Areas to Address

a. bases for comparison such as independent reports, company evaluations, laboratory testing, and benchmarks

b. current quality level comparisons with industry averages, industry leaders, and world leaders or other competitors in the company's key markets

c. current levels and trends in relation to the company's quality leadership objectives and plans. Explain adverse trends.

6.3 Business Process, Operational and Support Service Quality Improvement (35 pts.) Summarize trends in quality improvement, based upon key measures of business processes, operations and support services.

Areas to Address

a. trends in key operating quality measures for business processes, operations which produce the company's products and services, and support services

b. explain adverse trends and outline what steps the company has taken or plans to prevent recurrence

c. comparisons with industry averages, industry leaders and world leaders when such data are available. Briefly explain adverse indicators.

Note: *Key operating quality measures are the set of principal measurable characteristics of processes such as use of manpower, materials, energy and capital. Appropriate measures relate to lead times, yields, waste, inventory levels, rework of products and repeat of services, first-time success rates, environmental improvements, and other areas.*

6.4 Supplier Quality Improvement (30 pts.)   Summarize trends in improvement in quality of supplies and services furnished by other companies, based upon key measures of product and service quality.

Areas to Address

a. trends in key indicators of the quality of supplies and services. Briefly explain adverse trends.

b. brief explanation of current supplier quality and trends in terms of the company's key requirements and actions to improve supplier quality

c. highlight awards and recognition the company's key suppliers have received and the role the company played in helping suppliers improve their quality

7.0 Customer Satisfaction (300 pts.)

The *Customer Satisfaction* category examines the company's knowledge of the customer, overall customer service systems, responsiveness, and its ability to meet requirements and expectations. Also examined are current levels and trends in customer satisfaction.

7.1 Knowledge of Customer Requirements and Expectations (50 pts.) Describe how the company determines current and future customer requirements and expectations.

Areas to Address

a. process for identifying market segments, customer and potential customer groups, including customers of competitors, and their requirements and expectations through surveys, interviews and other contacts. (Include information on frequency, duration, objectivity, and depth of data collection and who collects such information.)

b. process for identifying product and service quality features and the relative importance of these features to customers or customer groups

c. cross comparisons with other key data and information such as complaints, losses and gains of customers, and performance data that may yield information on customer requirements and expectations and on key product and service features

d. how the company evaluates and improves the effectiveness of its processes for determining customer requirements and expectations such as improved surveys, other customer contacts, analysis, or cross comparisons

Notes: *(1) The buyer of a product or service may not be the end user. Thus, identifying customer groups needs to take into account both the buyer and the end user.*

(2) Product and service features refer to all important characteristics experienced by the customers, including delivery and after-sales service, that may bear upon customer preference and customer view of quality. These features also include the overall purchase and ownership experiences.

7.2 Customer Relationship Management (30 pts.)   Describe how the company provides effective management of its relationships with customers and how it ensures continuous improvement of customer relationship management.

Areas to Address

a. process for ensuring that customer service requirements are understood and responded to throughout the company

b. means for ensuring easy access for customers to comment, seek assistance, and complain

c. follow-up with customers on products and services to determine satisfaction and to gain information for improvement

d. empowering customer-contact employees to resolve problems promptly and to take extraordinary measures when appropriate

e. special hiring requirements, attitudinal and other training, recognition, and attitude/morale determination of customer-contact employees

f. technology and logistics (infrastructure) support to enable customer-contact employees to provide effective and timely customer service

g. analysis of complaint information, gains and losses of customers, and lost orders to assess costs and market consequences for policy review

h. process for evaluating and improving services to customers

7.3 Customer Service Standards (20 pts.) Describe the company's standards governing the direct contact between employees and customers, and how these standards are set and modified.

Areas to Address

a. selection of well-defined, objectively-measurable standards derived from customer requirements and expectations

b. employee involvement in developing, evaluating and improving or changing standards

c. deployment of requirements and/or standards information to all company units to ensure effective support for customer-contact employees who are expected to meet the company's customer-service standards

d. tracking to ensure that key service standards are met

e. how service standards are evaluated and improved

7.4 Commitment to Customers (20 pts.) Describe the company's commitments to customers on its explicit and implicit promises underlying its products and services.

Areas to Address

a. product and service guarantees and product warranties: comprehensiveness, conditions, understandability and credibility

b. other types of commitments the company makes to promote trust and confidence in its products and services

c. how improvements in the company's products and/or services over the past three years have been translated into changes in guarantees, warranties and other commitments

7.5 Complaint Resolution for Quality Improvement (30 pts.) Describe how the company handles complaints, resolves them, and uses complaint information for quality improvement and prevention of recurrence of problems.,

Areas to Address

a. process for ensuring that formal and informal complaints and critical comments made to different company units are aggregated for overall evaluation and use wherever appropriate throughout the company

b. process for ensuring that complaints are resolved promptly by customer-contact employees; summarize indicators of improved response including trends in response time

c. process for analyzing complaints to determine underlying causes and using this information to make improvements such as in processes, standards, and information to customers

d. process for evaluating the company's handling of complaints to improve both the response to complaints and the ability to translate the findings into preventive measures

7.6 Customer Satisfaction Determination (50 pts.) Describe the company's methods for determining customer satisfaction, how this information is used in quality improvement, and how methods for determining customer satisfaction are improved.

Areas to Address

a. types and frequency of methods used including procedures to ensure objectivity and validity

b. how satisfaction is segmented by customer groups, if appropriate, and how satisfaction relative to competitors is determined

c. correlation of satisfaction results with other satisfaction indicators such as complaints and gains and losses of customers

d. how information on key products and service quality features that determine customer preference is extracted from customer satisfaction data

e. how customer satisfaction information is used in quality improvement

 f. process used to evaluate and improve methods for determining customer satisfaction

7.7 Customer Satisfaction Results (50 pts.)   Briefly summarize trends in the company's customer satisfaction and in indicators of adverse customer response.

Areas to Address

 a. trends in customer satisfaction and key customer satisfaction indicators for products and services segmented by customer groups, if appropriate

 b. trends in major adverse indicators such as complaints, claims, refunds, mandatory recalls, returns, repeat services, replacements, downgrades, repairs, warranty costs and warranty work. Briefly explain adverse trends or data points.

Notes: *(1) Adverse indicators to be summarized in this Item relate to actions initiated by customers or on behalf of customers such as by government agencies or other third parties. Trends in adverse indicators where the action, such as recall or repeat service, is initiated by the company itself should be included in Item 6.1.*

(2) If the company has received any sanctions under regulation or contract over the past three years, include such information in this Item. Briefly describe how sanctions were resolved or current status.

7.8 Customer Satisfaction Comparison (50 pts.)   Compare the company's customer satisfaction results and recognition with those of competitors which provide similar products and services.

Areas to Address

 a. comparison of customer satisfaction results with industry averages, industry leaders and world leaders, or with other competitors in the company's key markets

 b. surveys, competitive awards, recognition and ratings by independent organizations including customers. Briefly explain surveys, awards, recognition and ratings.

 c. trends in gaining or losing customers. Briefly explain sources of gains and losses.

 d. trends in gaining and losing market share relative to major competitors, domestic and foreign. Briefly explain significant changes in terms of quality comparisons.

ORDERING GUIDELINES

Individual Copies

Individual copies of the 1990 Application Guidelines are available free of charge from:

Malcolm Baldrige National Quality Award
National Institute of Standards and Technology
Gaithersburg, MD 20899

Telephone: 301–975–2036

Telefax: 301–948–3716

Bulk Orders

Multiple copies of the 1990 Application Guidelines may be ordered in packets of 10 from:

American Society for Quality Control
Customer Service Department
310 W. Wisconsin Avenue
Milwaukee, WI 53203

Toll-Free: 800–952–6587
in Wisconsin: 414–272–8575
Telefax: 414–272–1734

Order Item Number T501;
Cost: $15.00 per packet of 10 plus postage and handling
    Postage and handling charges are:
      1 packet $ 3.50
      2–6 packets   5.00
      7 or more   10.00
For orders of 50 or more packets, the cost is $13.50 per packet.
For orders shipped outside of the continental U.S. and Canada, there is a fee of 25 percent of order value to cover postage and handling.

Payment

Payment options include check, money order, purchase order, VISA, MasterCard or American Express.
Payment must accompany all mail orders.
Payment must be made in U.S. currency. Checks and money orders must be drawn on U.S. institutions.
Make checks payable to the American Society for Quality Control.

Shipment

Orders delivered within the U.S. and Canada will be shipped UPS or first class mail. Special shipping arrangements can be made at time of order placement.

Standard Industrial Classification (SIC) Codes

Manufacturing and Products				Services			
Code	Sector	Code	Sector	Code	Sector	Code	Sector
01	Agriculture-crops	27	Printing and publishing	07	Agricultural services	60	Banking
02	Agriculture-livestock	28	Chemicals	40	Railroad transportation	61	Credit agencies
08	Forestry	29	Petroleum refining	41	Local & interurban transport	62	Security & commodity brokers
09	Fishing and hunting	30	Rubber and plastics	42	Trucking and warehousing	63	Insurance carriers
10	Metal Mining	31	Leather and leather products	44	Water transportation	64	Insurance agents
12	Coal mining	32	Stone/clay/glass/concrete products	45	Air transportation	65	Real estate
13	Oil and gas extraction	33	Primary metal industries	46	Pipelines/except natural gas	67	Holding & other investment offices
14	Mineral quarrying	34	Fabricated metal products	47	Transportation services	70	Hotels and lodging places
15	General building contractors	35	Machinery/computer equipment	48	Communications	72	Personal services
16	Heavy construction contractors	36	Electrical/electronic equipment	49	Electric/gas/sanitary services	73	Business services
17	Special trade contractors	37	Transportation equipment	50	Wholesale trade/durable goods	75	Auto repair and services
20	Food products	38	Instruments/clocks/optical goods	51	Wholesale trade/nondurable goods	76	Miscellaneous repair services
21	Tobacco products	39	Miscellaneous manufacturing	52	Retail building materials	78	Motion pictures
22	Textile mill products			53	General merchandise stores	79	Amusement and recreation
23	Apparel			54	Food stores	80	Health services
24	Lumber and wood products			55	Auto dealers & service stations	81	Legal services
25	Furniture and fixtures			56	Apparel and accessory stores	82	Educational services
26	Paper and allied products			57	Furniture stores	83	Social Services
				58	Eating and drinking places	84	Museum and art galleries
				59	Miscellaneous retail	86	Membership organizations
						87	Professional services
						89	Miscellaneous services

1989 AWARD RECIPIENTS

". . . all American firms benefit by having a standard of excellence to match and perhaps, one day, to surpass. For 1989 there can be no higher standard of quality management than those provided by the winners of the Malcolm Baldrige National Quality Award—Milliken & Company and Xerox (Business Products and Systems) . . ."

George Bush
November 2, 1989

Milliken & Company

Headquartered in Spartanburg, South Carolina, the 124-year-old privately-owned Milliken & Company has 14,300 "associates" employed primarily at 47 manufacturing facilities in the United States. Milliken's 28 businesses produce more than 48,000 different textile and chemical products—ranging from apparel fabrics and automotive fabrics to specialty chemicals and floor coverings. Annual sales exceed $1 billion.

In 1981, senior management implemented Milliken's Pursuit of Excellence (POE), a commitment to customer satisfaction that pervades all company levels. This pursuit has led to improvements in what most competitors had already considered an enviable record of quality and performance. Since the early 1980s, productivity has increased 42 percent.

Teams are a hallmark of the Milliken quality improvement process. In 1988, 1,600 Corrective Action Teams formed to address specific manufacturing or other internal business problems, 200 Supplier Action Teams worked to improve Milliken's relationships with its suppliers, and nearly 500 teams responded to the needs and aims of customers. Quality improvement measures are solidly based on factual information, contained in an array of standardized databases accessible from all Milliken facilities. Most manufacturing processes are under the scrutiny of real-time monitoring systems that detect errors and help pinpoint their causes. Milliken's successful push for quality improvement has allowed it to increase U.S. sales and enter foreign markets.

Xerox Business Products and Systems

In 1983, Xerox Business Products and Systems launched an ambitious quality improvement program to arrest its decline in a world market it had once dominated. Today, the company can once again claim the title of the industry's best in nearly all copier-product markets. The company, headquartered in Stamford, Connecticut, attributes the turnaround to its strategy of "leadership through quality." Through extensive data-collection efforts, Xerox Business Products and Systems knows what customers want in products and services. Planning of new products and services is based on detailed analyses of data organized in some 375 information management systems, of which 175 are specific to planning, managing, and evaluating quality improvement.

Benchmarking is highly developed at Xerox Business Products and Systems. In all key areas of product, service, and business performance, the company measures its achievement for each attribute and compares itself with the level of performance achieved by the world leader, regardless of industry.

Quality improvement and, ultimately, customer satisfaction are the job of every employee. Working with the Amalgamated Clothing & Textile Workers Union, the company ensures that workers are vested with considerable authority over day-to-day work decisions. Employees are expected to take the initiative in identifying and correcting problems that affect the quality of products or services.

Xerox Business Products and Systems employs 50,200 people at 83 U.S. locations. The company makes more than 250 types of document-processing equipment. U.S. sales exceeded $6 billion in 1988.

1988 AWARD RECIPIENTS

Globe Metallurgical Inc.
Motorola, Inc.
Commercial Nuclear Fuel Division of Westinghouse Electric Corporation

References

1. Danworth, Douglas D. "A Common Commitment to Total Quality." *Quality Progress* 19, No. 4 (April 1986): 15–17.

2. Larmin, Richard. "To Slow U.S. Decline, We Must Face It." *Fort Worth Star Telegram* 84, No. 102 (August 14, 1989): 11.

3. Kennedy, Paul. *The Rise and Fall of the Great Powers.* New York: Random House, 1987.

4. "Quality as a Means to Improving Our Nation's Competitiveness." House Republican Research Committee, Task Force on High Technology and Competitiveness. Washington, D.C. July 12, 1988.

5. "The Push For Quality." *Business Week* 3002, (June 8, 1987): 130–144.

6. Carlucci, Frank C. "A Quest for Excellence." Dayton, Ohio: Wright Brothers Chapter Speech, American Defense Preparedness Association. January 28, 1988.

7. Bette, John A. "Improving the Acquisition Process." City: Key Speeches, Aerospace Industries Association. September 1989.

8. Miller, Laurence A. *Barbarians to Bureaucrats.* New York: C.M. Potter, 1989.

9. Marsh, William A. "Management Theories: Comparing X, Y, and Z." *Quality Progress* 15, No. 12 (December 1982): 18–20.

10. Byrne, J.A., and Stewart Jackson. "Business Fads: What's In and Out." *Business Week* 2929 (January 20, 1986): 52–61.

11. Lowe, T.A., and J.M. Mazzoo. "Three Preachers, One Religion." *Quality,* 25 (September 1986): 32–37.

12. Talley, Dorsey J. "Managing Quality." Seattle: Boeing Commercial Aircraft Seminar. May 11, 1986.

13. Ingle, Sud. "Editor's Corner: Who Will Be the Next Industrial Power in Year 2000?" *QC Trends* 2, No. 3 (February 1986): 2.

14. "Managing Quality and Productivity in Aerospace and Defense." Fort Belvoir, Va.: Defense Systems Management College. December 1988.

15. Harrington, H. James. "A Guideline to Improvement." Tel Aviv: Israel Conference Proceedings, 11 May 1987. 7th Israel International Quality Conference.

16. Sedgwick, John. "Customers First." *Business Month* 134, No. 6 (June, 1989): 21–26.

17. Davis, Charles A. "Mismatched Signals Sound an Alarm." *Business Week* 3126, (October 2, 1989): 88–91.

18. Boyett, Joseph H., and Henry P. Conn. "Developing White-Collar Performance Measures." *National Productivity Review,* Summer 1988: 209–218.

19. Brown, Thomas A. "A Human Resource Credo." *Industry Week* 238, No. 18 (September 18, 1989): 23–25.

20. Talley, Dorsey J. "General Dynamics' QIP." Los Angeles: Mission Assurance Conference, May 11–13, 1983.

21. Hays, Herb C. "QIP Measures Survey." Ft. Worth, TX: General Dynamics, May 1985.

22. Kearns, David T. "Chasing a Moving Target." *Quality Progress* 22, No. 10 (October 1989): 29–31.

23. Walsh, Francis J., Jr. "Current Practices in Measuring Quality." Washington, DC: The Conference Board, Bulletin 224, 1989.

24. Harrington, H. James. *The Quality/Profit Connection.* Milwaukee: ASQC Quality Press, 1989.

25. Lubkin, Yale J. "The Roaring Mouse." *National Defense,* December 1988.

26. Daly, Charles R., Jr. "You're Flunking, Too!" *Industry Week* 238, No. 11 (June 5, 1989): 26–30.

27. Cox, Allan. "Achievers Lead by What They Do Best." *Industry Week* 238, No. 15 (August 7, 1989): 30–36.

28. Pascarella, Perry. "Visionary Leadership Will Design the Future." *Industry Week* 238, No. 16 (August 21, 1989): 15–19.

29. Burlingham, Bo. "Being the Boss." *Inc.* Vol. 11, No. 10 (October 1989): 48–65.

30. Livingston, Willie. "Potential Barriers to TQM." Forth Worth, Tex.: General Dynamics, August 8, 1989.

31. Weimerskirch, Arnold M. "Implementing Total Quality in a Multi-Divisional Corporation." Juran Impro '89. Atlanta, November 1, 1989.

32. Kandero, Stanley W. "U.S. Leaders Cite Need for National Technology Plan." *Aviation Week* 131, No. 14 (October 2, 1989): 27–28.

Suggested Readings

The key to effective and successful TQM implementation is understanding the underlying philosophy and theories supporting continuous improvement efforts. It is also imperative that we continue to pay close attention to history. The critical relationship between economics and military power directly affects the survival of nations.

Crosby, Philip B. *Quality Is Free*. New York: McGraw-Hill Book Co., 1979.

Deming, W. Edwards. *Out of the Crisis*. Cambridge, Mass.: Massachusetts Institute of Technology Center for Advanced Engineering Study, 1986.

Feigenbaum, Armand V. *Total Quality Control*. New York: McGraw-Hill Book Co., 1983.

Harrington, H. James. *The Improvement Process*. Milwaukee: ASQC Quality Press, 1987.

Kennedy, Paul. *The Rise and Fall of the Great Powers*. New York: Random House, 1987.

Juran, Joseph M. *Leadership for Quality*. New York: Free Press, 1989.

Juran, Joseph M. *Managerial Breakthrough*. New York: McGraw-Hill Book Co., 1964.

"Managing Quality and Productivity in Aerospace and Defense," Defense Systems Management College, Ft. Belvoir, Va., December 1988.

Ouichi, William. *Theory Z*. Menlo Park, Calif.: Addison-Wesley Publishing Co., 1981.

Talley, Dorsey J. *Management Audits for Excellence*. Milwaukee: ASQC Quality Press, 1988.

INDEX